COACHING THE LITTLE LEAGUE®

HITTER

TEACHING YOUR PLAYERS
to Hit with Skill and Confidence

JOHN MONTELEONE

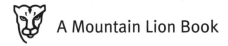 A Mountain Lion Book

McGraw·Hill

New York   Chicago   San Francisco   Lisbon   London   Madrid   Mexico City
Milan   New Delhi   San Juan   Seoul   Singapore   Sydney   Toronto

Library of Congress Cataloging-in-Publication Data

Monteleone, John J.
    Coaching the little league hitter / by John Monteleone.
        p.   cm.
    ISBN 0-07-141791-5
    1. Hitting (Baseball).   2. Baseball for children—Coaching. 3. Little League
baseball.   I. Title.

    GV871.M66   2004
    796.357′62—dc22   2003016999

2 3 4 5 6 7 8 9 0   AGM/AGM   3 2 1 0 9 8 7 6 5 4

ISBN 0-07-141791-5

Interior photographs by Barry Havens

McGraw-Hill books are available at special quantity discounts to use as premiums and
sales promotions, or for use in corporate training programs. For more information, please
write to the Director of Special Sales, Professional Publishing, McGraw-Hill, Two Penn
Plaza, New York, NY 10121-2298. Or contact your local bookstore.

This book is printed on acid-free paper.

This book is dedicated to the great players and coaches who have shared their insights and understanding of the art and science of hitting. These include Andy Monteleone, my dad, who first showed me how to take two and hit to right; Steve Braun, this book's resident hitting guru and keen observer of all that thousands of swings will reveal about the mechanics of hitting; Tom Wilson, natural teacher and hitting coach extraordinaire; the late Charley Lau, major league baseball's hitting instruction pioneer; Jack Tracy, Seton Hall University's storied baseball program's toughest out and greatest competitor; Chuck Doehler and Owen Carroll, Seton Hall University's gentlemen coaches of low-key, high-yield insights; Tom Seaver, Baseball Hall of Fame pitcher; and Tony Oliva, three-time American League batting champion, who showed that rhythm has an application beyond the dance floor.

Contents

Acknowledgments

This book was conceived and developed by Mountain Lion, Inc., a book producer that specializes in instructional and general reference books in the sports category. A book producer brings together and relies on the special skills of many individuals. The following contributed to developing and producing *Coaching the Little League® Hitter*, and to all of them, "Thank you."

Tom Wilson, researcher/writer and youth league baseball coach, who assisted in writing the text and coordinated all the tasks of taking the photographs for the book.

Steve Braun, New York Yankees minor league batting coach who teaches hitting to players of the Trenton Thunder, a Yankees affiliate in the Eastern League (AA), who contributed special insights and tips for young hitters, which are sprinkled throughout the book under the heading "Coach's Box: Steve Braun Says . . ."

Kevin Wilson, special consultant of Kevin Wilson Baseball, who contributed portions of the text, including some of the special skill-building drills.

Don DeAngelis, who arranged for use of the Little League baseball field in Washington Township, New Jersey, in order to take the instructional photographs.

Acknowledgments

Coaches Steve Braun, left, and Tom Wilson, right, instruct Little League player Ryan DeAngelis.

viii

   Ryan DeAngelis and Kevin Dragert, who demonstrated the drills and skills depicted in the photographs. Their batting skills are so fundamentally sound that our photographer had very few retakes. Way to go, guys!

   Barry Havens, photographer, who took all the photographs that illustrate the text.

   Matthew Carnicelli, editor at McGraw-Hill, and Craig Bolt, editorial team leader, who shepherded the project for the publisher.

For Coaches and Parents: How to Use This Book

This book is intended not only to teach young players the basics of hitting but also to help parents and coaches who want to help young players improve their hitting skills. The simplest way for parents and coaches to get involved with the help of *Coaching the Little League Hitter* is to (1) read and thoroughly digest the instructions set forth in each chapter, (2) assist with the drills, and (3) chart the player's progress.

Read and thoroughly digest the instructions. In other words, get on the same page with the young hitter when you go to assist him or her. Hitting is not rocket science. Nearly every interested adult can learn the techniques and then observe and compare what's prescribed on these pages with what the hitter is showing. Troubleshooting, that is, identifying faults and prescribing the necessary adjustments, will involve some trial and error and false starts, but stick with it. Follow along with all the information, recheck it when you spot a problem with the hitter, and then return to one of the recommended drills to get the hitter back on track. If the cure is not here, use your imagination to develop a new drill to solve the problem.

Assist with the drills. Players need assistance in performing many of the recommended drills. A teammate, coach, or parent of the aspiring batsman can provide this. Make it fun. Put games and little contests into the drills and batting practice. This will keep the player coming back for more and keep up his enthusiasm during practices.

Many of the drills call for the use of a batting tee. If you don't already have a batting tee, buy one. It is a year-round hitting aid and a good investment.

Chart the player's progress. Players like feedback on their performance. Drills are usually not very glamorous and often tedious, but they also offer the opportunity to track a player's skill building. Where applicable, keep records, even a diary, and use your records to show the player how he's improving. You can also use the unique grading system, "What's Your Hitting Quotient?," that is provided in the Appendix of this book. It provides a simple, foolproof system for grading a hitter's skills. The form grades each player on his basic setup, through swing and follow-through, eye-hand coordination, and ability to hit line drives (quality at-bat).

Hitting is a skill that is best learned away from the heat of competition. Don't coach or provide tips during a player's turn at the plate. When the player is batting, keep it simple. Let him concentrate on following and hitting the ball. Afterward, there will be plenty of time to go over the player's offensive game and individual plate appearances. Wait at least 24 hours to begin correcting any mistakes you observed. Always coach the player one-on-one in a tension-free situation. One last consideration—whenever you're using live batting practices, that is, you're throwing pitches to a batter, insist that the player wear a batting helmet for safety.

Note: The use of masculine-gender pronouns—"he," "his," and "him"—in this book is strictly for the sake of convenience. No offense is intended toward those girls or women who might pick up and read this book in search of the secrets of hitting.

Introduction

Be yourself.

At home or in school you have probably heard this advice. In terms of baseball, "be yourself" means to recognize your abilities and potential, set reasonable goals, and then pursue those goals. In other words, don't try to be someone you're not.

This approach is especially important when it comes to hitting. The type of hitter you'll eventually become depends on several factors, such as your size, weight, strength, speed, and reflexes. Most importantly, it depends on your awareness of these factors in yourself and your willingness to work with them, not against them. Inherited genes play a significant role in physical development—a factor beyond the player's control. Who knows what your genes may grow you into? If you grow no taller than the legendary Yogi Berra and you have the forearms of Popeye, you may very easily develop into a power-hitting catcher. Again, accept who you are, and develop your own style and objectives accordingly.

As you mature, your physical development may dictate a different style of hitting and different goals. A Little League hitter may not be the same type of hitter when he reaches high school or college. Adjust as your physical attributes and skills mature. For example, a very young player who possesses good speed and the ability to spray the ball through and over the infield might evolve into a very strong teenager and young adult who is capable of consistently hitting the ball with power.

The point is this: young players should not worry about who they will eventually become; instead, they should concentrate on the fundamentals of hitting and just try to hit hard line drives. Don't worry about home runs at age 10, regardless of what size you happen to be. Trying to hit home runs in your early years prevents you from learning the basic swing mechanics and serves only to delay your progress as a hitter.

Part of being yourself also applies to your stance and mannerisms, especially those individual tics or movements that reduce tension while waiting for the pitcher to release the pitch. Although this book suggests a particular stance that is productive for the young player, it doesn't rule out the possibility that a player will eventually create a style of his own that is equally effective. Major league baseball has always been filled with players whose stances are strikingly different in one way or another. Joe DiMaggio, for example, used a very wide stance. When asked early in his career if anyone ever tried to change his stance, Joe said, "Why would anyone want to change a player who's hitting .500?" He had a good point. He set his feet wider apart than most hitters yet still applied all the fundamental elements of a good swing. Therefore, you don't necessarily have to fit into a certain mold, as long as you perform the key elements of the swing correctly.

Pete Rose knew early in his adult life what kind of hitter he was destined to be. Pete was a switch-hitter who hit mostly singles and doubles while using his speed, hustle, and competitive nature to run the base paths as aggressively as anyone who has ever played the game. He was quite content to forgo trying to hit home runs in exchange for becoming the all-time leader in base hits.

Players can even change after arriving at the major league level. Take Barry Bonds, for example. As a leadoff hitter in his early years with the Pittsburgh Pirates, he was not a pure power hitter. His role was to get on base, steal bases, and score runs—all of which he did extremely well. Later in his career, however, he transformed into a power hitter who hit cleanup for the San Francisco Giants and broke Mark McGwire's single-season home run record. Barry's transformation occurred in midcareer. Garrett Anderson of the 2002 World Champion Anaheim Angels is another player who developed his hitting skills in stages. After first establishing himself as a competent all-around hitter at the major league level, he then added power and the ability to drive in runs.

Another example of a player who knows his role and developed it is the five-foot, six-inch, 170-pound David Eckstein of the 2002 World Champion Anaheim Angels. He is proof that there's a place for players who have a unique batting style and set of batting skills as long as they can be productive. David chokes the bat, crowds the plate, and works deep counts. He has a knack for getting on base, either by scratching out a hit, bunting, walking, or getting hit by a pitch. Once on base, he is a threat to steal a base and run the bases aggressively, taking an extra base when he can. Plus, he makes the plays in the field at both second base and shortstop. Although David may not fit the mold of today's bigger and stronger player, he is a hustler who understands and applies his strengths, knows his role in creating runs, and almost always gets done what the situation calls for. To many, he is a throwback, a player who resembles the style and characteristics of players in the early eras of baseball when few runs were scored with one swing of the bat.

Unusual circumstances can also play a factor in a player's development. For example, the sandlot where Baseball Hall of Famer Stan Musial played as a youngster had an unplayable right field. Any ball hit there would be lost in a water-filled trench. As a left-handed hitter, Stan had to learn to hit every ball to center field and left field. This proved to be an invaluable skill that enabled him to become a feared major league hitter who could hit the ball to all fields with power. He would likely not have been such a versatile hitter had it not been for that sandlot experience.

The following chapters explain 10 steps toward consistent hitting. They represent 10 of the most important and fundamental concepts that hitters should master. The steps are presented in sequential order—starting with the grip and ending with the follow-through. It is recommended that you read all 10 in that order, rather than skipping around, because each chapter builds upon the prior chapter. Perform the drills and become comfortable and satisfied with your performance of each chapter's instructions before moving on to the next chapter.

Each chapter includes advice and insight from Steve Braun, New York Yankees minor league batting instructor. Braun played in the major leagues for 15 years with five teams. He ranks eighth on the major league all time pinch-hitting list. Braun was a member of the 1982 World Champion St. Louis Cardinals.

Braun has spent nearly two decades as a minor league batting instructor for the St. Louis Cardinals, Boston Red Sox, and now the Yankees. He has coached many major league players including Nomar Garciaparra, Shea Hillenbrand, Trot Nixon, David Eckstein, Mo Vaughn, Todd Zeile, and Ray Lankford. Braun has been a student of hitting nearly all his life and enjoys sharing the knowledge he has acquired through his years of experience working with professional as well as youth baseball players.

Little League players are not expected to completely master all the principles of hitting explained in this book. These skills require hours of repetition over several years to master. The best players learn, practice, and improve a little each day. Instead, use this book to become aware of correct hitting mechanics so that you can immediately begin practicing the skills that will make you a better hitter at an early age. In other words, acquire good habits now so that you won't need to correct bad habits later. Refer to this book even after you've advanced beyond the Little League level.

Each player brings his own physical attributes, talents, and style to the field. A player can maintain his individuality while staying true to the rules of hitting as presented in this book. Imagine if all major league hitters looked alike at the plate. Their creativity and innate skills would be wasted; they would not "be themselves."

As you begin reading the hitting ideas in the following chapters and incorporating them into your swing, watch major league players more closely and find these techniques in their swings. When you can recognize these elements in others and see how they work for them, you'll be even more confident that you can make these techniques work for you.

THE FINGER PRESS

Getting a Good Grip

> *As long as you've got a grip that is comfortable and that allows you a maximum amount of flexibility, you'll be fine.*
>
> —Charley Lau

Charley Lau, the legendary hitting instructor, said in his book, *The Art of Hitting .300*, that the grip is an important part of the baseball swing. In teaching the grip he suggests you use a grip that is firm, relaxed, and comfortable. A "death grip"—that is, one in which a batter grips the bat so hard his knuckles turn white—brings on tension that doesn't just stay in the hands. It works its way up, tightening the muscles in the forearms, the biceps, and shoulder muscles until the player is tense all over. So an overriding rule of thumb is not to hold the bat as if your life depended on it.

The Grip

So how do you grip the bat properly yet not squeeze the handle so hard it's reduced to sawdust? Try the following. Place the bat handle in the area of the hand between the palm and fingers, at the base of your fingers. Make sure your fingertips touch the bat; you should be able to see a little bit of the bat handle near your fingertips. If you select a bat with a large bat handle, the bat will rest more in the palm than against the base of the fingers. Therefore, choose a handle whose diameter or circumference (in general terms, its thickness) is small, maneuverable, and comfortable. This is especially important for very young players whose hands have not yet developed or for those players who have exceptionally small hands.

Some people believe that the knuckles of both hands should be directly aligned when gripping the bat. This is not a good idea, however, because it reduces flexibility, movement, and power, and it feels awkward. The most comfortable and effective alignment for a young player is to align the middle knuckles of the top hand between the second and third set of knuckles of the bottom hand. This should put the bat at the base of the fingers of both hands, not in the palms of the hands. As the player gets older and develops, he may alter this a bit through experimentation.

Here is an easy way for players to make a proper grip. As you approach the plate, drop the barrel end of the bat on the ground and rest the handle end against your leg. Then grab the handle with both hands while leaving the barrel end on the ground. Let the handle rest along the base of your fingers. Wrap your fingers around the bat, aligning the middle knuckles of the top hand between the second and third set of knuckles of the bottom hand. Be sure both hands touch each other, allowing no space between them so they can work as a unit. Lift the bat off the ground and up to your shoulder. Then examine the grip to make sure it is properly aligned and the bat is not in your palms. This procedure should be done while in the on-deck circle before each at-bat and each time you step into the batter's box.

Again, it is okay to look at grips of major league players and notice the variety and differences, but be sure to choose a grip that meets your needs based on your age, size, and strength.

Choke Up Versus End Grip

Power hitters often place their bottom hand at the bottom of the handle, against or near the knob. This creates a wider arc in the swing and increased speed of the barrel. Some major leaguers even dangle the pinky finger off the end of the bat, as Mickey Mantle did. This obviously works for them, but it is not recommended for young players because it can cause you to lose bat control. Young players need to concentrate on hitting the ball consistently, not hitting tape-measure home runs. Therefore, if you elect to hold the bat near or at the end, leave a small gap (a half inch) between the knob and hand. Choking up on the bat three or four inches creates a shorter swing arc, thus less power, but it creates better bat control and more consistent contact with the ball. You will see major leaguers choking up with two strikes on them. This gives them greater bat control in order to make contact, avoid the strikeout, and get the ball in play. Choking up gives you the confidence to do that.

3

Choking up is not just for singles hitters or batters with two strike counts. Some of today's power hitters choke up one or two inches. Barry Bonds is an excellent example. He is certainly strong and powerful, but choking up gives him greater control of the bat head, the added dimension that improves his consistency.

By choking up at least an inch or two, young players can develop and improve their swings more rapidly and make contact with the ball more often. They should not be afraid to choke up, worried

Leave a half-inch gap between the knob and your hands.

Choking up on the bat three to four inches gives better bat control.

4

that others may think of them as weak. That is hardly the case. Just ask Barry Bonds.

Tension Is the Enemy

Consider tension as the enemy and never let it interfere with your swing. It is okay to be intense—that is, focused completely on each pitch. However, that intensity should not produce tension in the hands, which can easily spread to the rest of your body, including your mind. Tension restricts your movements and reduces bat speed, power, flexibility, and the whip action in your swing. It impairs your thought process. When your mind is frozen by tension, it does not transmit messages to your body as quickly; thus your body's response to a pitch is slowed.

When standing in the batter's box, relax and hold the bat loosely. Envision a scale of 1 to 10 that measures the firmness of your grip. Ten is the highest degree of firmness. You wouldn't hold the bat at a rating of 1—it would fall out of your hands. And you wouldn't hold it at 10, what famed batting coach Charley Lau called "the white-knuckle syndrome"—you'd squeeze so hard you would drive the blood out of your fingers and quickly tire your hands, arms, and shoulders. Hold it somewhere in between, say, 7 and 8.

Lifting your fingers off and on the bat can keep you from freezing. The time to tighten the grip is when the pitch is being delivered. Don't worry; you will automatically tighten the grip when you see the pitch on its way. At that point you won't have any conscious thoughts of how firmly you're gripping the bat. Your natural instincts and athletic skills will take over—you'll simply grip the bat firmly enough to move the bat head through the hitting zone.

Lifting your fingers off and on the bat can keep you relaxed.

Let your muscles relax until it is time to put them to use. If you exhaust them in advance, they won't be able to supply their full power and energy when needed. If you find yourself feeling tense, relax and let the tension drain from your body through a chain reaction. Your mind and body react much better when relaxed.

Here is a basketball analogy. Think of shooting a potential game-winning free throw with one second remaining on the clock. If you become filled with tension while standing at the free-throw line, you lose the natural fluidity in your movements, your arm extension shortens, and your confidence erodes. In contrast, think of shooting in a relaxed state—just like in practice. Apply that same approach to hitting. Take a deep breath. It not only brings in a rush of oxygen, which helps your muscles to work, but it releases the tension in your body. That's what gives you the best chance for success. It is your choice, so choose to be relaxed.

BAT WEIGHT

The weight of the bat is an important consideration in obtaining a comfortable grip. The bat should feel perfect in your hands. If the bat winds up seated in the palms of your hands, it is a sign that it is too heavy, that you need the extra support from the palms to get the bat around—or even to pick up the bat. If you can comfortably lift the bat off the ground with the majority of the weight in your fingers, then you have found the perfect bat.

Here is another way to make sure your bat is not too heavy. Put one hand on the end of the handle, with pinky finger on the knob. Lift the bat and extend it out in front of your body and up to shoulder level. Hold the bat with your palm facing down. The bat now becomes an extension of your arm, creating a 90-degree angle between the bat and your body. If you cannot hold this position for 20 seconds, the bat is too heavy for you.

With pinky finger on the knob, lift and hold the bat in front of your body for 20 seconds.

Top Hand Versus Bottom

The top and bottom hands work together. Start this partnership by applying equal pressure with each hand. While waiting for the pitch, you can keep a good feel of this pressure by milking the grip, that is, continually and rhythmically lifting and resetting the fingers on the handle. World-class golfer Sergio Garcia milks his grip before hitting a shot to keep relaxed and focused on the shot he intends to hit.

Though the hands work together, each also carries out a distinct task. The top hand directs the head or barrel of the bat toward the ball and changes the course of its path when necessary. The bottom hand pulls the bat through the zone (with the help of a rotating torso), whereas the top hand pushes it through the zone. The top hand is capable of propelling the barrel ahead of the hands as it moves through the hitting zone, which creates an angle of contact that sends the ball to the batter's side of the field. However, if the hands are too tightly wrapped on the handle, they cannot react as quickly, and they are not effective in getting the bat head to the ball in time to drive the ball anywhere deep into fair territory.

If a player allows his top hand to dominate the swing he usually pulls the ball more. For example, hitting legend Ted Williams, a left-handed, pull hitter for whom a shift was created in which three infielders played on the second base side of the infield, was successful despite seldom hitting the ball to the opposite field. In Ted's case, his top hand was dominant and he pulled the ball, even if the pitch was on the outside corner.

Despite the infielders' shift and Ted's determination to pull the ball, Ted hit .406 in 1941. It's no wonder many consider him the greatest hitter of all time. But just think what his average might have been if he had hit to all fields using a less dominant top hand.

Drill

The purpose of this drill is to become comfortable with the correct grip through repetition. All you need is your coach to pitch to you. First, select a bat that is the proper weight, as described earlier in this chapter. Grip the bat correctly: place the bat handle at the base of your fingers; align the middle knuckles of the top hand between the second and third set of knuckles of the bottom hand; and hold the bat loosely. Take 20 swings at pitches thrown by the coach, making sure to regrip before each pitch. Then, to experience the difference, place the bat handle back in your palms, with knuckles aligned and a tight grip. Take a few swings and note the inflexibility, reduced bat speed, and awkward feeling. Then grip the bat correctly again and continue hitting, remembering to regrip before each pitch. Through repetition you will eventually grip the bat correctly without even thinking about it. This is the goal.

COACH'S BOX Steve Braun Says . . .

Here's how to set the fingers and hands on the bat correctly.

Younger players often have smaller hands, which makes it difficult to find a bat that fits comfortably. In most cases they will find it easier to make the proper grip if they use a bat with a thin handle. It may be difficult to find a bat with a thin handle, but parents should try to get the best possible fit for their youngsters.

There is a specific way I show players how to pick up a bat so their fingers and hands fall correctly into place. First, I set the barrel end of the bat on the ground with the handle pointing up. Then I lay the bat handle across my hands. When I look down, the handle should lie across the top hand where the knuckles of the last three fingers meet the palm of the hand and across the middle knuckle of the forefinger. Then I do the same with the bottom hand, letting the thumb come around and touch the forefinger. When I lift the bat, I can see the fingertips pressing against the bat.

The fingertips are the most sensitive part of the hands; therefore, to maintain maximum control of the bat, the fingertips must be in contact with the handle. Fingertip contact with the handle allows you to maneuver the bat and gives you a feel of the bat head. Think about this for minute. When a surgeon holds a scalpel in his hands, he holds it with his fingertips. This gives him better control. If the surgeon were to hold it in the palm of his hand, he wouldn't be able to control it as well.

Here are two important points about using the proper grip. First, when you lay the bat across the fingers, it enables the thumb pad of the top hand to get behind the ball as you bring the bat forward and make contact. This promotes solid contact and transfers more energy into the ball, while effectively absorbing the energy produced by the ball. In contrast, if the bat is resting in the palm of the hand, the

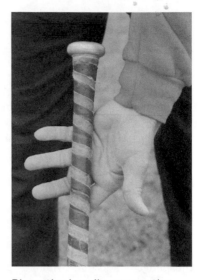

Place the barrel end of the bat on the ground with the handle pointing up.

Place the handle across the top hand where the knuckles of the last three fingers meet the palm of the hand and across the middle knuckle of the forefinger.

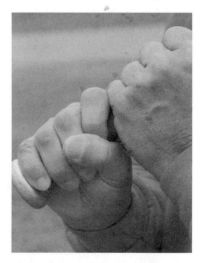

The thumbs wrap over the forefingers.

You should see the fingertips pressing against the bat.

energy is transferred into the soft tissue between the joints of the thumb and forefinger. This transfers less force into the ball and produces a weaker swing. Second, gripping the bat too far into the palms raises the barrel of the bat prematurely into an early or premature follow-through. It doesn't allow the barrel to stay on plane through the hitting zone as long as is necessary to achieve solid contact.

The sooner a player learns the proper grip the sooner it becomes a habit. Remember, whatever grip you repeatedly apply—whether correct or incorrect—becomes comfortable simply because you're accustomed to it. A player who

11

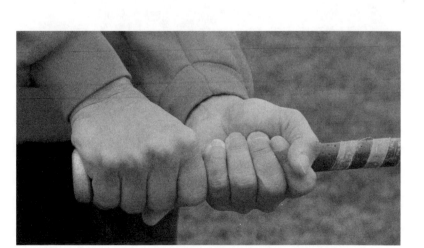

The thumb pad of the top hand is behind the ball on contact.

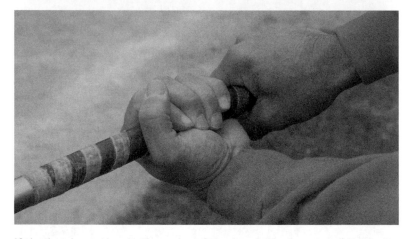

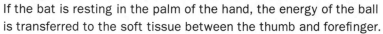

If the bat is resting in the palm of the hand, the energy of the ball is transferred to the soft tissue between the thumb and forefinger.

repeatedly holds the bat in the palms of his hands becomes comfortable with what is really an incorrect grip. Many of the players I've coached, when faced with a grip correction, say, "That doesn't feel right." This is because they've become comfortable with the feel of their grip through repetition, even though it is incorrect.

Old habits are hard to break, so it's important to learn the correct grip at an early age.

Play It Again, Sam

- Mastering the correct grip is merely a matter of daily practice and repetition until it becomes automatic.
- The recommended grip for a young player: place the bat handle between the palm and fingers, at the base of your fingers—not in the palms of your hands or deep in your fingers.
- Do not directly align your knuckles when gripping the bat. Instead, align the middle knuckles of the top hand between the second and third set of knuckles of the bottom hand.
- By choking up an inch or two you will make contact more often and improve your hitting more quickly.
- Relax and hold the bat loosely. Tension is the enemy; it can quickly spread through your body and mind. Tension robs your muscles of the strength needed for your swing. It also restricts your movements and reduces bat speed, power, and flexibility.
- Choose a bat that is not too heavy. A heavy bat will find its way to the palms of your hands.
- The top hand guides the bat and pushes it through the hitting zone. The bottom hand pulls the bat through the zone.

2

YOU AIN'T JUST STYLIN'
The Athletic Stance

> *Balance means being in a good, comfortable position at the plate.*
>
> —Tony Gwynn

One common thread in all of sport is the athletic stance. It is the foundation upon which all movements and performances are built. Picture a defensive back in football as he waits for the snap. His body assumes a stance that enables him to follow the pattern of the wide receiver. A basketball player uses a defensive stance that lets him respond quickly to the deceptive moves of his opponent. Similarly, the hitter benefits from an athletic stance. In the hitter's case, he needs to react quickly to a ball thrown from a relatively short distance.

Comfort and balance are the most important factors in selecting a good stance. Eventually, you should develop your own stance based on your size, athletic ability, and what feels most natural to you. Recognize your particular qualities as a player, and don't automatically copy the stance of a teammate or a major league player.

Be yourself. But at a young age it is wise to use a basic stance.

The Basic Stance

Your first concern is comfort and balance. Begin with a basic or square stance that gives you the best chance for initial success. Copying or trying anything unusual or awkward will only add to the difficulty of hitting, which is already hard enough. In fact, Ted Williams frequently referred to hitting a baseball as the single most difficult thing to do in sport.

So, what is the best stance for a young player? Follow these steps:

16

- *Spread your feet slightly beyond shoulder-width apart.* This lets you easily shift weight back and forward while maintaining good balance. If your feet are too far apart, you may have problems shifting your weight, striding correctly, and rotating your hips. If they are too close together, you will have difficulty in maintaining balance. After setting up in your stance, use the following method for verifying that your feet are at least shoulder-width apart. Place your bat perpendicular to the ground and against the inside of your back or pivot foot. If the bat aligns with your hip bone, the width of your stance is correct. If the bat is markedly outside your hip, your stance is too wide. If the bat is closer to your spine than outside the hip, your stance is too narrow. Adjust your stance and repeat the test.
- *Square your feet to the pitcher.* This aligns the toes of your feet on a line that is parallel to the closest edge of the plate, or along a line that runs straight to the pitcher. You are more

Spread your feet slightly beyond shoulder-width apart.

When the bat aligns with your hip bone the width of your stance is correct.

If the bat is significantly outside your hip your stance is too wide.

If the bat is close to the spine the stance is too narrow.

Square your feet to the pitcher.

likely to stride straight toward the pitcher from this square position. You are also able to focus both eyes on the pitcher.

- *Evenly distribute your weight on the balls of your feet.* This promotes good balance and allows you to move quickly. A Charley Lau tip: by bending at the waist and then bending your knees, your weight should automatically shift to the balls of your feet.
- *Bend your knees slightly.* This gets you into the ready position, allowing your body to move freely. It gives you a sense of balance and athleticism necessary to be a successful hitter.
- *Bend over slightly at the waist.* This prevents your weight from shifting back on your heels.
- *Keep your back straight.* Don't bend over too much. Envision an outfielder's ready position; now, just picture a bat in his hands and place him in the batter's box.

- *Align your shoulders to the pitcher.* Keep your head level and fix both eyes on the pitcher.
- *Raise your hands to shoulder height and align them with the inside of your rear shoulder.* The idea is to start your hands where they don't have far to go to get to the hitting position.
- *Keep your hands four to six inches away from your body.* If your hands are too close to your body, you will have difficulty extending them in time to meet the ball. If they are too far, you reduce bat speed and the ability to hit to all fields

Bend your knees slightly.

19

Fix both eyes on the pitcher.

Raise the hands to at least shoulder height.

Keep the hands four to six inches away from the body.

20

(you will tend to swing out and "around the ball" and thus pull it more often).

As you gain playing experience and your body develops, you can alter this basic stance to fit your specific needs. But regardless of the stances you use in your baseball life, the stance should always feel natural—never like you are straining to force your body into a mold that isn't the right size. In addition to being comfortable, it must be effective so that you can produce a good swing. Don't sacrifice efficiency for style; you don't get points for style, only for base hits. As you define the type of hitter you are (for example singles hitter, power hitter, slap hitter), your stance will be formed to meet the requirements of that type of hitter.

Other Considerations
Plate Coverage

Stand close enough to the plate to make sure you can reach a pitch on the outside corner with full arm extension. You don't want to stand so close to the plate, however, that you get jammed by an inside pitch and you can't get the meat of the bat on the ball. Also, if you are too close, you will likely step in the bucket (a right-handed hitter steps toward third base) to hit the inside pitch on the sweet spot. This is an awkward maneuver that drives your body back rather than through the ball.

Determining the proper distance from the plate is not an exact science; it requires some experimentation. But first, think about your physical makeup. Are you tall? Do you have long or short arms? Also, consider the length of your bat. Add these things to the equation. Experiment with the distance you think may be best, and then put it to the test during batting practice.

Begin by standing in the middle of the batter's box.

Up or Back in the Box?

Begin by standing in the middle of the batter's box. Keep in mind that the farther back you stand the more time you have to see the pitch. This can be helpful if you have trouble getting the bat around in time to hit the fastball. On the other hand, if you're facing slower pitches or breaking balls then step up in the box. You will still be able to catch up to the fastball (of mediocre speed), and you'll hit the breaking pitches before they curve very far. In most cases, however, it is best to take your stance in the middle of the box.

Bat Angle

While in your stance, hold the bat somewhere between vertical and horizontal; a 45-degree angle is a

Hold the bat somewhere near a 45-degree angle.

A flat or horizontal position promotes the fault of going around the ball.

A vertical position takes extra time to reposition the bat for the downswing.

good compromise. Know that the greater the angle, the heavier the bat feels. In other words, the vertical angle makes the bat feel lighter than when held horizontally. The 45-degree angle also promotes a level swing. Again, this choice is a matter of comfort. Look in the mirror to get a feel for the angles. You will eventually want to be able to sense the angle of the bat without requiring a mirror.

The Dirt

When you enter the batter's box, examine the dirt for evenness. Smooth out any rough spots and fill in any depressions or holes. Make sure that the landing area for your front foot is level. You may want to dig a small indentation to give your rear foot a place from which to push off. Make the box conform to your needs before getting into your stance.

Common Stances

Although the basic or square stance is favored for young players, it is worth describing the three most common stances: open, closed, and square. As you develop physically and gain experience, knowledge of these stances may help you refine your swing based on what you discover about yourself as a hitter.

Open

In the open stance, the rear foot is closer to the plate than the front foot. This stance lets you face the mound and more easily focus both eyes on the pitcher. It allows your hips to open and rotate more easily, which increases bat speed and helps you get the bat around to pull the inside pitch. With the open stance, however, you must be careful to align your front foot with the pitcher as you stride; otherwise, you will pull off the ball and not hit it on the meat of the bat. In other words, there is a tendency to step in the bucket with an open stance. Although the open stance is good for pulling the inside pitch, it may make it more difficult to hit the pitch on the outside corner.

23

Closed

In the closed stance, the front foot is closer to the plate than the rear foot. This stance makes it easier to hit to the opposite field because your lead foot steps toward the plate. It can also be of help to hitters who are trying to avoid the habit of stepping in the bucket. However, this stance can make it more difficult to pull the fastball on the inside corner with-

In an open stance the rear foot is closer to the plate than the stride or front foot.

In a closed stance the front foot is closer to the plate than the rear or pivot foot.

In a square stance the feet are aligned with the pitcher and equidistant from the plate.

out being jammed. The closed angle can also restrict your view of the pitcher.

Square

The square stance, sometimes called the even or parallel stance, which was introduced earlier as the basic stance, is often the preferred variation for young players because it gives you the best plate coverage, good balance, and the shortest approach to the pitch. The feet are perfectly aligned along an imaginary line that runs straight to the pitcher. Young players benefit greatly from this stance because it increases the probability that the front foot will stride directly toward the pitcher, a technique that must be learned at the very beginning. It also makes it easier to keep your weight on the balls of your feet, thus maintaining good balance. And it allows you to pull the inside pitch as well as hit the outside pitch to the opposite field. With the square stance, both eyes are on the pitcher.

Be aware that the open and closed stances present advantages and disadvantages. They can provide solutions for older players who must contend with several types of pitches (such as the curveball or slider) and delivery angles that young players don't see. Therefore, the best suggestion for a young player is to keep it simple and use the square stance.

HOW FAR SHOULD YOU SPREAD YOUR FEET?

If you're not sure how far you should spread your feet in the stance, here is something to try. Stand in the batter's box with your bat on your shoulder. Jump straight up in the air to a fairly good height. Upon landing, don't move your feet until you note the distance between them. They are probably going to be a little more than shoulder-width apart. Your mind and body's natural inclination is to land in a position that provides the best support and balance.

Jump in the air and use the distance between your feet upon landing as your stance width.

Drill

Stand in front of a full-length mirror with bat in hand. Slowly assume each of the elements of the basic square stance. Look in the mirror and use the steps described earlier as a checklist. Then begin a rhythmical preswing routine to remain loose. Seek the comfort and balance that are so important to your stance. Once you feel confident about your stance, step away for a moment, then step in front of the mirror and repeat the process. Do 10 repetitions.

COACH'S BOX Steve Braun Says . . .

You need to have consistent plate coverage.

Here is a simple technique for determining where to stand in the batter's box to obtain the best plate coverage. First, take your stance in the box at a distance from the plate that feels correct. Then, without taking a stride, simulate the beginning of the swing by rotating your hips and pulling your hands down and inside to your belt buckle. Hinge your hands—that is, move them into the impact position with the bottom hand palm down, top hand palm up—and bring the bat barrel forward so that it is perpendicular to the pitcher. Now look to see how much of the barrel is covering the plate. The end of the bat should reach the outside back edge of the plate and the sweet spot should cover the center of the plate. If the bat is not in this position, reposition your feet to obtain this coverage.

Stand slightly back in the box with your front shoulder about even with the rear corners of the plate. After you've established your feet in the proper position, assume a fairly erect stance with your knees bent slightly. Next, fully extend the bat with your bottom hand only toward the far back corner of the plate and drop the barrel end of the bat onto the plate. Pay attention to where the end touches the

Pull your hands down alongside your belt buckle.

Bring the bat barrel forward so it is perpendicular to the pitcher.

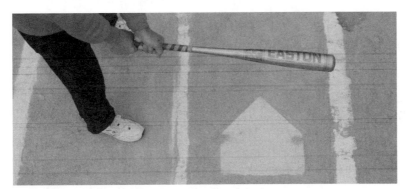

The sweet spot should cover the center of the plate.

plate. It may strike the plate exactly on the far corner or touch the ground beyond it, or it may fall somewhere on the plate itself or perhaps on a spot of dirt alongside the edge of the plate. It doesn't matter, as long as you mentally mark the spot and use it to set up each time you step into the batter's box.

Drop the barrel end of the bat onto the back point of the plate.

This technique will enable you to consistently confirm plate coverage just by taking your stance and dropping the bat—one arm extended—toward the opposite corner of the plate. This works with any stance, in any batter's box and in any ballpark, regardless of what the batter's box looks like.

As stated earlier, I'm a firm believer that the even or parallel stance (also called the square stance) is the best variation for young players. It allows both eyes to focus on the pitcher, and it offers the best chance for the front foot to move straight ahead to the pitcher.

The closed stance (front foot closer to the plate than the rear foot) requires the batter to compensate for his irregular bodylines and make adjustments to return to the fundamental swing motions.

The open stance (rear foot closer to the plate than the front foot) creates similar problems as the batter tries to move back into the direction of the pitch. As a result, the eyes move and focus is disrupted. In my opinion, the extreme open or extreme closed stance gets too far away from the fundamentals of the swing. However, if a player feels he must use the open or closed stance for some reason, he should not make it too extreme.

In these instances, the feet should not be more than half a foot-length behind or in front of the other. Again, I strongly recommend the neutral or even stance for young players.

The angle at which the hitter holds the bat while waiting for the pitch is another important factor. I recommend holding the bat midway between flat and vertical (close to a 45-degree angle) because it allows you to drop the bat directly down into the slot and inside the ball, which is the first phase of the swing. The bat moves more quickly to the ball and there is less chance for error. If the angle is too flat, it causes an outward swing—like casting a fishing line. If the angle is vertical, an extra move is required to get the bat to the 45-degree angle before pulling it down into the slot. You can't swing directly from a vertical or flat position because before the bat goes down to the ball it has to get into the 45-degree angle. It makes good sense to start the bat at or near the 45-degree angle that launches the swing. Not only does it get the bat forward and down quickly, it gives the batter a little more time to see the ball before starting the swing.

29

Hold the bat at a 45-degree angle.

Drop the bat directly down into the slot and inside the path of the ball.

Play It Again, Sam

- The athletic stance is used in all sports.
- Seek comfort and balance in your stance.
- Young players should start with the basic stance.
- As the player matures and the level of pitching improves, adjustments may be made to the stance to meet specific needs.
- Stand close enough to the plate to hit the pitch on the outside corner, yet far enough away to avoid being jammed by an inside pitch.
- Three common stances are the open, closed, and square stances. The square stance gives young players the best chance for success.

3

HAPPY FEET ARE FOR DANCING, NOT HITTING

Balance and Movement

> *When you're dead in the box—no movement—it requires more energy to get something going than having some movement, some rhythm in the box.*
>
> —Wade Boggs

Establishing a balanced stance in the batter's box is important. So is maintaining that balanced stance until the pitch arrives. You can do this when you create some form of rhythmical motion; however, certain actions, especially ones that have too much movement, can be detrimental to your swing.

Happy Feet Syndrome
What Is It?

Think of your feet as forming a grounded, rock solid base—a source of strength from which your body generates a swing. Let nothing compromise this foundation, especially "happy feet," that peculiar, yet common phenomenon among young players. Hitters who repeatedly move their feet before and/or during the pitcher's delivery are referred to as having "happy feet." As an example, a batter steps into the box and sets up in a good stance. Everything looks good so far; then his feet start traveling. One at a time, his feet lift slightly off the ground—or maybe just his heels. Pretty soon he is jumping around the box as if he is stepping on hot coals, destroying his nicely balanced stance. And more often than not, the feet are still moving when the pitch arrives—which is a definite "no-no."

32

Happy feet move back and away from the plate.

Cause

Happy feet are often a sign of nervousness, anxiety, tension, and a lack of confidence. These Nervous Nellies send a message to the pitcher that "this guy is not setting up in the box to do some business, so he must be an easy out," thus increasing the pitcher's confidence. As you approach the plate, the decision is yours: either look like a confident hitter and gain the advantage, or give the advantage to the pitcher by your display of anxiety. The batter must look and feel confident when he walks up to the plate; he can't let the pitcher think he is going to be successful, and that there's an automatic out stepping into the batter's box.

Problems

Here are some problems caused by happy feet:

33

- Dancing feet make it difficult to maintain balance and control of your lower body, thus undermining the effort you put into establishing a balanced stance.
- It is difficult to keep your weight on the balls of your feet; weight can easily shift back to your heels or forward onto your toes.
- If your feet are in midstep (in the air) while the pitch is on the way, your timing and weight distribution will most likely be out of kilter.
- Your power is reduced. Since your legs are a source of power, the dancing robs them of a firm foundation from which to stride and rotate the hips.
- You lose the sense of timing. Your fidgeting may leave one foot in midair when the pitch is delivered, rather than both feet firmly in position on the ground. Too much is left to chance.
- The distance between your feet and their position in the box may be altered significantly from your original stance.

To remedy happy feet, try flexing the knees more than normal.

34

Remedies

If happy feet plague you, here are some remedies. First, make sure that you use a good, balanced stance, as described in Chapter 2. Then try bending your knees a bit more than normal. The more you bend your knees, the harder it is to dance. Dig in your back foot and keep it firmly planted. You should visualize your feet as the firm foundation upon which your swing is created.

Because tension is a contributor to happy feet, try releasing that tension by stepping out of the box (to the side) with the front foot. Keep your back foot planted firmly in the box, take one or two deep breaths, and let the tension flow out of your body. Next, bring the front foot back into place

Release tension by stepping out of the box.

and assume a natural, athletic stance. Channel any remaining nervousness into a controlled and very slight movement forward and back. You can do this by slowly pressing down alternately on the inside of each foot and gently rocking back and forth. This relaxes you and creates the timing, energy, and balance required for a smooth transition into the swing. Perception is important. Let everyone see that you are in control, cool, and con-

fident—even though you may still have some anxiety. Look confident and you'll feel confident.

Balance and Movement

Remember that once you are set up in your balanced stance, it is
important to remain loose and prevent your muscles from tightening. In addition to moving your body in a slow, rhythmical fashion
forward and back, try slowly swinging the bat forward and back
in pendulum fashion below the waist. This will not only relax you
but also keep your hands and wrists loose. This motion should continue until the pitcher begins his windup.

Picture a tennis player waiting for his opponent to serve. He is
in the athletic stance, rocking left and right, while keeping balance
on the balls of his feet. He is fully prepared and focused to react to
the serve. Similarly, the batter should rock forward and back in a
comfortable and controlled motion with eyes and head stable.

35

What are the benefits of this controlled movement?

- It is easier to start the swing
  from a body slightly in motion than from a frozen position. Sam Snead, one of the
  greatest golfers of all time,
  preached the value of a subtle
  nudge forward with the lower
  body (without moving the
  feet), followed by the start of
  the golf swing.
- It prepares you to naturally
  move into the swing and generate the momentum for your

Slowly swing
the bat
forward and
back below
the waist.

weight shift toward the ball. You stride to the pitch with more authority, confidence, and power.

- Movement serves as a timing mechanism for the start of your swing.
- Motion helps you maintain good balance on the balls of your feet.
- It prevents your body and mind from freezing up.
- It raises your level of concentration and helps you see the ball better.

Developing an effective preswing movement is strictly an individual matter. Your goal is to create a rhythmical movement that is natural and easily repeatable. It may be helpful to think about patterning your motion with the help of a metronome or simply using a verbal count system. If you've learned to softly shift your weight from instep to instep you can say to yourself in cadence, "Back, forward, back, forward," and thus time the ever-so-slight back-and-forth movements so that when the pitcher is releasing the ball you are "back"—that is, ready to start the swing with approximately 70 percent of your weight distributed over the back leg.

When the pitcher is releasing the ball, have approximately 70 percent of your weight on your back leg.

Just don't get carried away and out of control, making your efforts counterproductive. Style and flare won't necessarily get you where you want to go. Efficiency of motion is essential. Eliminate any excess movement that doesn't contribute toward your goal. Experiment to find a personalized preswing routine that fits your needs.

BECOME YOUR OWN COACH

To a certain extent, a hitter can become his own hitting coach. That's quite a statement! Of course, this does not suggest that a player should ever ignore the help and instruction of coaches. It merely implies that a player who acquires a sufficient understanding of the principles that form a good swing can then critique his own swing, diagnose problems, and prescribe remedies. This is particularly helpful when he is practicing on his own or is alone in the batter's box during a game.

Therefore, a young player who is serious about baseball should strive to become his own coach. But this does not happen overnight. It requires a thorough education in the mechanics of hitting and a lot of self-study. Take Tony Gwynn, for example. He looked at film of his swing taken from various angles every day during the course of his career to find flaws and make improvements. He was a true student of hitting and studied the swings of many great hitters over the years. Although Ted Williams did not have the benefit of such film in his era, he knew his swing inside and out and was happy to share his theory with fellow players or anyone who cared to listen. If you are a serious player, the study of hitting can be fascinating; but best of all, with every new bit of information and technique you acquire, you move another step toward becoming your own hitting coach.

37

Drill

To feel the difference between a swing that starts from a still position versus a body in motion, try this drill. Place a ball on a tee and get into a balanced stance. Then take a hard swing at the ball from a still position—dead in the box. Do this a couple of times. Next, step up to the tee and start a smooth, rhythmical motion forward

Take a hard swing from a rhythmical back and forward motion.

and back with your body and bat. Take a hard swing. Do this a couple of times. You should notice the momentum gained from your motion as you shift your weight into the ball, resulting in more power. You should also feel more loose, flexible, and relaxed.

COACH'S BOX Steve Braun Says . . .

Waggle while you wait.

Every hitter should develop his own rhythmical preswing motion that promotes relaxation and good timing. Your most relaxed standing position is when your arms are down to your side, as when walking down the street. Therefore, lower your arms during your preswing motion and slowly waggle your bat forward and back—similar to the waggles of Mark McGwire or Jason Giambi. A waggle can start a

Slowly waggle your bat back
and forth below the waist.

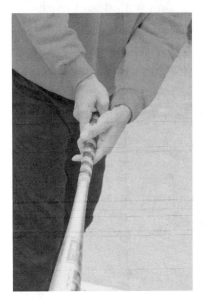

chain reaction of good hitting habits: it promotes relaxation, which creates rhythm, which leads to a slow step or stride forward, which leads to good balance and a strong hitting position.

Keeping your mind on the waggle gets your mind off other things. Tony Oliva, my former teammate on the Minnesota Twins and one of the best hitters of his era, kept up a small amount of movement while in the batter's box, and his swing just flowed from that movement. He never locked up because he kept moving.

I remember attending a grade school dance where one of my teachers noticed that I wasn't dancing. He approached me and told me that dancing would give me balance and teach me rhythm, which would make me a better hitter. I gave it a try, and he was right. Keeping time to the music and learning to dance with rhythm improved my timing as a hitter.

Play It Again, Sam

- Create a rhythmical motion with your body and bat while in the batter's box. This helps you to remain loose and to maintain a balanced stance. Plus, it is easier to start the swing from a body in motion than from a frozen position.
- Avoid "happy feet"—that is, shuffling your feet or lifting them up and down while in the box.
- Eliminate happy feet by bending your knees and releasing tension with deep breaths.
- Look confident when entering the box to gain an advantage over the pitcher.
- Eventually, learn enough about hitting mechanics so you can become your own batting coach.

4

LOCK AND LOAD

How to Shift Your Weight and Separate

> *You can't go forward unless you go back first.*
>
> —Charley Lau

At first glance, this statement by Charley Lau may seem odd. But when considered in the context of the swing, it makes good sense. It means that the batter's weight should go back toward the catcher before he shifts it forward to hit the ball. This is a part of the swing commonly known as "loading up." In contrast, most young hitters move immediately toward the pitch from a dead stop—often moving their hands first. This reduces bat speed and adversely affects quickness when bringing the barrel of the bat to the ball and overall timing.

Loading Up

Analogies for loading up are numerous. For example, a pitcher doesn't throw his best fastball from a neutral body position, with his weight centered. Instead, he rears back and fires. That is, he shifts his body weight to the rear when his arm starts back. That weight shift, or loading up, is what allows a pitcher to gather the momentum to go forward, which increases the speed of his pitches.

A common hitting fault is to move or "carry" the hands forward along with the upper body and stride foot.

42

A golfer also shifts his weight back before making a forward thrust through the ball. Ted Williams calls it a pendulum action. Regardless of how you term it, or in what sport you observe it, loading up is all about creating power.

How Does Loading Up Occur?

Loading up must be preceded by a balanced stance and rhythmical motion as described in Chapters 2 and 3. This prepares you to shift your weight back with good balance and rhythm. Here's how to load up, shift weight, and separate:

1. Position your head so that your chin is resting over and slightly behind your front shoulder. This focuses both eyes forward, slightly closes the front shoulder, moves the bat back into a position of four to six inches in front of the rear shoulder and slightly above the top of the strike zone, and keeps the hips aligned toward the pitcher.

2. Just before the pitcher starts his windup, lightly bounce your weight to the rear until 60 to 70 percent of your weight is on your back leg. Then gently bounce forward to your 50/50 (evenly balanced) position. Repeat this until the pitcher starts his windup. This motion serves as a timing mechanism and helps to make sure that your first move is back, not forward, when the pitch is delivered.

Position the head behind a slightly lowered front shoulder.

43

Lightly bounce your weight to the back leg.

Gently bounce your weight forward to a 50/50 weight distribution.

3. When the pitcher is in his windup, slowly move your weight back to your rear leg so that 60 to 70 percent of your weight is on the back leg. Be careful not to sway your body back so far that you lose balance.

4. As the pitcher brings his arm forward to the point of the hand's release of the ball, simultaneously stride forward with your front foot approximately four to six inches while moving your hands back approximately one to three inches; this is called "separation." This separation allows you to cock your wrists, which in turn will increase your bat speed through the hitting or contact zone when the hands fire the bat head. Don't wrap your hands too far around behind your rear shoulder where they will get "trapped." Don't move your hands too far straight back so that the arm "bars," that is, becomes locked at the elbow in full extension. From either of these positions, the hands won't be able to move the barrel of the bat forward quickly enough to meet the ball at the proper contact point.

44

Separation: hands back, stride foot forward.

Trapped hands arrive late in the hitting zone.

Don't tilt your body upward when you load up. Keep the shoulders at a slight angle downward toward the pitcher. A tilt upward usually results in an uppercut. Instead, keep your hips parallel with the ground; let your head and front shoulder follow the near-level or level position of your hips.

A barred arm produces a slow, sweeping swing.

Core Strength

Power is generated from the torso, which plays a key role in positioning the hands and arms in the swing. At the start of your movement toward the ball, your torso brings your hands forward into the correct position (the hitting zone). The bat stays close to your body as the torso moves forward; this prevents your hands from extending out too far and making an elongated swing. Instead, the bat takes a direct path to the ball.

The torso moves slightly forward until the stride foot plants (first the toe touches the ground and then the heel goes down). The stride leg absorbs the lateral (or forward) movement either in a straight, firm position or in a slightly bent (at the knee) position. Then the hips rotate, fully when the stride leg is straight and not quite as fully when the leg is slightly bent. For a right-handed batter, think of getting your belly button to the pull side of the pitcher on a full rotation and to the second base side on a partial rotation. To get an idea of how a full rotation looks, watch slugger Jim Thome. For a partial rotation watch Derek Jeter when he hits a ball to the right side of second base.

As the hips rotate, the knob of your bat will point toward the ball as it enters the hitting zone. Your hands take over from this

45

For a right-handed hitter, think of getting your belly button on the pull side of the pitcher (pointing at the short-stop) on a full rotation.

46

point and propel or fire the bat head through impact, extension, and follow-through.

Your back hip is essential in striking the ball. After loading up and separating, rotate your back hip toward fair territory. This does two things: it generates the power from your torso, and it moves your hands into a perfect position to strike the ball. The explosive movement of Barry Bonds is a perfect example. He shifts his weight back, getting himself in perfect position to attack the pitch. From that loaded position he takes a short stride, then rotates his hips and creates an explosive swing that generates power to all fields. His upper body has a part in the swing, but it merely follows his torso. Without hip rotation, his upper body doesn't create maximum power. His upper body automatically reacts to—and follows in close sequence—whatever his torso does.

The body functions as one unit. Whatever the lower half does, the upper half has to follow. That's just how it works!

Benefits

Loading up serves as a timing mechanism. When the pitcher's arm starts back, you begin shifting weight back to be in sync with him.

The weight shift onto your front foot is more powerful when it starts from the rear foot, rather than from a central or neutral position.

The value of loading up is nothing new. Consider this statement made many years ago by the legendary Branch Rickey: "No man who starts his swing from halfway back achieves the full limit of his acceleration. This man will have no power." Mr. Rickey was a player, manager, and general manager in the major leagues. He is perhaps best known for elevating Jackie Robinson from the minor leagues to the Brooklyn Dodgers in 1947, thus breaking the color barrier in major league baseball.

How to Build a Controlled Stride

Here is an exercise that can help you keep from moving too far forward during the stride, and help you make a controlled yet powerful stride into the pitch. While in your balanced stance, place a stick or draw a line in the dirt (in the direction of toe to heel) that splits the distance between your feet in half. Stand a bat, barrel down, on this line. If extended upward, the line or stick would dissect the middle of your stomach and head, splitting your body in half. This represents a point at which you should work to keep both the starting and finishing point in your stride. To do this successfully, it is not necessary to finish with your belly button precisely on the line you've drawn in the dirt. But by keeping it as close as possible you will train yourself to make a quiet, controlled stride.

Here are some goals to shoot for: After you shift your weight back (load up) in preparation to swing, keep your body pretty much centered or just slightly behind that line. Similarly, when you move forward toward the ball, keep your body at or close to the line in the dirt at the completion of your swing. This enables you to keep the majority of your weight on your back leg and inside the back hip during the forward movement, which enables you to utilize your whole body during the swing.

Drill

A bat and tee are needed for this drill. First, establish a balanced stance. Draw a line in the dirt splitting the distance between your two feet. Place your chin over your front shoulder. Gently bounce your weight to your back leg (from 50/50 weight ratio to 60/40 or 70/30), and then softly bounce back to center. Be careful not to rock back and forth excessively; make it a subtle and rhythmical bounce. Now, bounce back again, and then stride forward while simultaneously bringing your hands back (separation). Repeat. Do this a third time, but this time hit the ball off the tee. Try to keep the center of your body aligned with the line in the dirt throughout the swing.

Note: Whenever hitting off a batting tee, place the ball on the tee with the narrow portion of the seams facing the catcher. Hit the seam that is closest to you. In order to hit the inside seam, your hands have to be inside the ball. This means that your hands are close to your body when they approach the hitting zone. As a result, you should be hitting balls up the middle and to the opposite field.

Keep your body centered throughout the setup and swing.

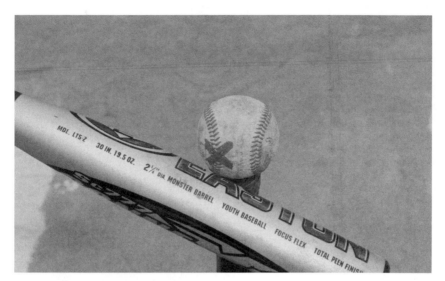

Hit the seam that is closest to you.

COACH'S BOX Steve Braun Says . . .

Approach the ball softly and slowly.

One of the most important elements of the approach to the ball is the pace or speed at which it is done. The softer and slower you approach the ball, the easier it is to control the upper body and maintain balance. But the faster the stride, the faster the upper body must react to keep pace. You need to shift your weight back early enough to enable you to make that slow stride. If you don't, the stride quickens and every subsequent movement accelerates in order to catch up, thus disrupting the entire timing sequence. When the body begins to move too fast, it causes the head and eyes to move. Focus becomes distorted and the ball appears to be traveling faster than it really is.

Lunging at the ball is a natural inclination for youngsters. Because they're not strong enough, they use the forward movement of their body to help them swing the bat. This causes the problem of striding and swinging at the same time. During your approach to the ball (stealth stride), only your front foot should move forward. The upper body, which moved backward when the stride began, will come forward to some extent when the stride is completed. But the head should not go past the midline of the body and the hands should stay back in the loaded position. After you complete the stride and you have maintained upper body control, you should look very much like you did in your stance. This puts you in a very strong position to start the swing.

Early in his career, Baseball Hall of Famer Ozzie Smith had a problem with his upper body—he was advancing it too far forward onto his front leg during his stride. This was a lunging problem. To correct this he focused on controlling the core of his body, that is, his back, abdomen (stomach), and hip muscles. During and after completion of his stride he imagined a rod through the center of his body, that is, along the line of his spine, touching the ground directly between his feet. It worked for Ozzie, it can work for you.

Another way to prevent lunging is to imagine your head staying over your back leg while striding. In reality, this is not physically possible (the head tends to stay centered over the upper body), but it is a useful overcorrection, as it will keep you from lunging. This also helps to keep the front foot from stepping away from the pitcher (in the bucket).

When Jason Giambi first came up to the major leagues and I got to see his swing, I liked his stride and approach to the ball. I could tell he would become a good hitter. He made a stride with his toes closed and body squared, and he made a slow, calm approach to the ball.

Hitting coach Gary Ward's comparison of the major components of the swing to a car's four-speed transmission is very useful. He feels that the stride and approach to the ball represent first gear—your swing, like a car, starts slowly. Second gear is the uncoiling action of the hips and torso—it transfers energy to the body from the ground up. Third gear of the swing is when you fire the back muscles and bring the bat down into the slot, or angle of approach to the ball. The back

Prevent lunging by imagining your head staying over your back leg while striding.

51

muscles pull and triceps muscles of the upper arms extend. Fourth gear is the action of the hands and wrists. By the time you hit fourth gear everything is moving, you're at maximum speed, and the bat head is flying through the hitting zone.

Play It Again, Sam

- Your weight should go back before you shift forward to hit the ball. This is called "loading up."
- To load up, transfer 60 percent of your weight onto your rear leg, but don't sway back so far that you lose balance.

- To separate, simultaneously stride forward with your front foot while moving your hands back slightly; don't move your hands too far back or wrap them around your shoulder.
- The movement of your torso forward brings your hands and bat into the hitting zone. From there, your arms take the bat through impact, extension, and follow-through.
- Draw a line in the dirt dissecting the middle of your body. Try not to move the center of your body too far off that line throughout your swing.

5

THE SNEAK ATTACK
How to Make the Stealth Stride

I like to keep the stride as short as possible. Six inches is fine. When you stride too far your whole body goes forward. The shorter the stride, the better you can stay back.

—Ryne Sandberg

Several years ago a major league batting coach videotaped a game in which a mirror-and-camera setup allowed the viewer to see both the batter and pitcher at the same time. This produced a split-screen image and made it clear that every batter begins to react when the pitcher has his arm almost completely extended, just before he releases the ball.

It also showed that every batter reacts differently. If at the key moment, the batter moved his upper body either up or forward instead of starting to stride with his front foot, he had a poor swing. However, if the batter's first reaction was to shift his weight back and then move his front foot forward (without moving his body in that direction at the same time), his swing was generally pretty good.

This shows that moving back as part of your rhythm, then striding forward with your front foot without bringing the bulk of your body along with it works best. This is what we call the "stealth stride," so named because we want you to think of the soft, quiet stride or step toward the pitcher almost as a "secret" move, one that is so quiet and short (four to six inches at most) that it is hardly noticeable. Think of it as sneaking up on the pitcher.

The Stride

The stride begins after your weight has shifted to your back leg (60/40 or 70/30 percent), as described in Chapter 4. As the pitcher is about to release the ball, stride slowly with your front foot

Stride is a stealthy four to six inches.

Think of it as sneaking up toward the pitcher.

directly toward him. This gives you the most options in the event you need to adjust to the direction of the pitch. Stepping out takes your body away from the plate and makes you vulnerable to the pitch on the outside corner. Stepping in toward the plate closes your stance and allows you to get jammed on an inside pitch. Overstriding lowers your eyes and makes it difficult for your eyes to focus.

As you stride, keep your front toe closed; that is, point it toward the plate in the same

Stepping away from the plate makes you vulnerable to pitches on the outside corner.

55

Stepping toward the plate makes you vulnerable to getting jammed on inside pitches, particularly fastballs.

Overstriding lowers your eyes.

parallel position as in your original stance. This enables you to land on the ball of your foot, helping to maintain balance. If your toe opens to the pitcher, you land on your heel, causing your hips to open too soon, and you lose power. Come as close as you can to keeping your toes closed when you land.

Land softly, as if you are stepping onto a pond's thin ice. A soft landing is easier when your weight is back. A heavy landing tends to bring your weight forward prematurely, disrupting your timing and shifting your eye level up and down. Only your front foot and leg move forward. About 60 percent of your weight still rests on your back leg when your front foot lands. Your hands and bat should also be back in the launching position at this time.

After the ball of your foot touches ground, your front heel touches down. Your hips then begin to rotate and your hands start to come through. Your front leg is slightly bent at impact, and then it quickly stiffens like a post to accept and control your weight transfer in a balanced manner.

After striding and placing your foot down, your head should still be in the middle of your body—not forward or back. Advancing your head or upper body toward the pitch too fast or too far disrupts your vision, making it difficult to focus.

Advancing your head or upper body disrupts your vision and focus.

Here is another important point about the stealth stride: a hitter must step first and swing second. Successful hitters always step and swing. They don't try to do both at the same time. And they never step to swing; that is, they don't try to pick up the location of the pitch—inside or outside—and then step toward that area. It is humanly impossible to do this successfully. There simply is not enough time. You have only four-tenths of a second from the time the pitcher releases the ball until you must strike it with the bat, and you have less than two-tenths of a second to swing after you have recognized the pitch. Remember, you must step first and swing second.

Players who don't step first and swing second have difficulty generating power. They make contact but hit weak grounders or fly balls. Here's why. When a player starts his swing as he steps, he brings his hands forward and slightly uncoils his body and shifts his weight too soon onto the stride foot or leg. This causes the front leg to bend at the knee or buckle slightly—the result is that you cannot use the leg as a foundation for rotating your hips and firing the bat through the impact area. You've lost the ability to drive the ball with power. Think of it this way: if you want your bat to show some pop, it's the forward motion of your body that you must stop!

Overstriding

Longer strides can disrupt your balance and timing, diminish your strength and power, and cause you to swing underneath the ball; your head and eyes lower during the long stride and you lose focus on the ball. Also, the longer the stride, the greater the tendency to bring your hands forward too soon, making it more difficult to hit off-speed pitches and pitches up in the strike zone.

Be aggressive, but don't lunge at the ball. Lunging causes the upper body to go too far forward too fast; it is not a balanced move. Your stride should also be slow; this results in fast hands. In contrast, a quick stride gets you off balance and slows down your hands. Remember that by striding you help the ball get to you more quickly by shortening the distance. So, the longer the stride, the less time you have to react to the ball and the more likely that your bat will be late getting into the hitting zone.

A long stride can make your head bob, making the pitch appear to jump in and out of your vision. And the long stride can make it difficult to rotate fully on the inside pitch, resulting in getting jammed—your feet are too far from the center of your body and it's hard to get the bat out in front. Next time you get a chance to watch Boston Red Sox All-Star shortstop Nomar Garciaparra bat, look for his unique "stealth stride." It is so quiet and small that he merely lifts the heel of his stride foot and places it back down when the pitcher delivers the pitch.

HITTING A BASEBALL VERSUS HITTING A GOLF BALL

You may be familiar with hitting a golf ball. Some people say that hitting a baseball is a lot like hitting a golf ball. Well, the answer is "yes and no." Many of the things you do when hitting a baseball you do when you hit a golf ball. For example, you shift your weight and rotate your hips. The launch positions of the golf and baseball swings are similar; that is, you start moving the barrel of the bat and head of the golf club with the hands held at about shoulder height over the rear shoulder.

But there are many important differences. For one, the golf ball is not a moving target. A baseball can be hit to all fields—left, center, and right—and still be in play. A golf ball that is hit to the left or right of the target is often out-of-bounds (out of play) or a long way off line (left or right) of the target. Unlike baseball, in golf you have to play your "foul balls."

However, the most important distinction is timing. Both swings require proper timing—that is, bringing the club head or barrel of the bat to the ball at the moment that brings the best results. But in baseball a hitter must strike instantly, many times when his mechanics are out of sync. Remember, one of the pitcher's goals is to upset the hitter's timing. He does this by throwing pitches at various speeds, or pitches that change elevation and direction—that is, drop or swerve. Often, the hitter has to swing at a pitch after his weight has shifted too soon (often on a change-up or slow pitch). To compensate, he uses fast hands, which fire the barrel of the bat through the impact area with enough speed to drive the baseball into the outfield.

In golf, instant speeding up of the hands is not as important. Because the ball is stationary and the golfer uses a rhythmic motion, there is plenty of time for the body to shift its weight forward, rotate the hips, and bring down the arms and hands in an unhurried sequence of motions. A golfer can even stop his swing when going back or coming forward—as Tiger Woods has demonstrated many times. But a hitter is tracking a pitch at a high speed moving in unpredictable ways, and he must bring the barrel of the bat to the ball with swift hand action.

59

If you mix your golf and baseball, remember that staying in rhythm is important to both swings but that golf allows you the time to bring the club forward at your own pace. With the baseball swing you must allow for the pitcher's deception and desire to upset your timing, and you must compensate with rapid movement of the hands.

Here is one bit of advice on keeping your hands ready for the instantaneous action that is required: Plan to swing at every pitch. Gear all your hitting actions—up to and including the stealth step—to swing until you decide not to swing. In other words, use what was recommended earlier—step and swing. Keep your hands back until you decide if you are going to swing. If you do, bring them forward with the bat as fast as you can.

Drill

This drill requires a bat and someone to act as a pitcher. Take a balanced stance in the batter's box. Place a bat on the ground four to six inches in front of and parallel to your front foot. Ask a coach or teammate to assume the role of pitcher on the mound. As the pitcher begins his windup, load up (shift 60 percent of your weight onto your back foot). As he is about to release the ball (simulation only), slowly stride forward straight toward the pitcher and separate (bring your hands back) at the same time. Land softly on the ball of your foot with your toe closed. Don't let your foot touch the bat on the ground. Feel your weight and hands back and your head centered as you land. Don't swing the bat. Just feel the stride elements. Repeat this 10 times with the pitcher simulating a thrown pitch. Then repeat 10 more times with the pitcher actually throwing the ball. Still don't swing. Just stride.

COACH'S BOX Steve Braun Says . . .

Separate—and then swing.

"Separation" is the toughest phase of hitting for players to learn— even at the professional level of baseball. Separation occurs after the batter has shifted his weight back (loading up). He then creates separation by striding forward with his front foot while moving his hands back at the same time. Many young players tend to stride and swing at the same time, which prevents them from controlling their body weight and reduces their power. By striding and swinging at the same time they've already committed to the swing and carried their hands forward. This does not provide enough time to see the location of the pitch or determine what kind of pitch it is. This phase of the swing should be the time for this recognition to occur.

When separating, be careful not to bring your hands so far back that you bar (fully extend) the arm of your bottom hand. Your hands should only move slightly back during separation. If you bar your arm, you'll most likely swing outside the ball and sweep at it, rather than using your hands in the swing. Baseball Hall of Fame sluggers Harmon Killebrew and Mickey Mantle frequently barred their arms, but they were so strong they could get away with it.

One of the biggest obstacles in learning separation is that players do not understand that it's an action made up of two phases. It's a "one-two" count. On the count of one, the stride foot moves forward with the toe or ball of the foot touching the ground with about 70 percent of the weight still over the back leg while the hands simultaneously slide backward a couple of inches or more. (Viewed from the side, the hands move to the back from the torso and the stride foot separates to the front from the torso—which is why it's called separation.) The hips remain closed. On the count of two, the front

A barred arm slows down your swing and makes you vulnerable to inside pitches.

The first phase of hitting moves the stride foot forward and hands back; the second phase has the stride foot fully planted, the hips rotate, and the hands start down and forward.

foot fully plants itself down (heel and ball), the hips start rotating open, and the hands start forward. In a swing with no separation, batters start their hands forward before their front foot lands. As a result, they swing while they stride and they shut down their power source—the legs, hips, and torso—from the beginning.

If a player just can't learn to separate, it may be useful to try "precocking," which means to shift his weight and hands back and foot forward (in the position where it would land upon striding) and leave them there while the pitcher is winding up. The Red Sox's Nomar Garciaparra does this successfully. When he swings, Garciaparra quickly drops the heel of his stride foot and executes a powerful swing aided by a rapid hip rotation. Just remember that once you're back in the precock position, there is no room for any additional shift backward without going off balance.

I have a theory about what makes separation so difficult for some youngsters to master. It centers on the use of pitching machines that release the ball from a spinning wheel. Fastballs suddenly spew forth from these machines without any warning because there isn't any arm action involved. Players need to develop a sense of timing—weight back, stride, and separate—that only comes from seeing the arm action prior to release. It is far better to practice hitting off live pitching or at least machines with mechanical arms.

Play It Again, Sam

63

- If a batter moves back and then forward with his stride foot without moving the bulk of his body forward, he is in a good position to swing.
- The "stealth stride" is short and quiet—that is, done with minimal body motion.
- Make a short (four to six inches) stride, landing softly on the ball of your foot with toe closed (facing the plate).
- Long strides can disrupt balance and timing, reduce power, and cause you to swing under the ball.
- Successful hitters step first and swing second; they don't step and swing at the same time.

6

THE BARRY BONDS MOVE

Staying Closed, Exploding Open

Your hips lead your hands through the zone, not the other way around. Your power comes from your legs.

—Dusty Baker

Many young players commonly believe that their arms and hands generate all the power in the swing. They don't think about how other parts of their body play important roles. In reality, a powerful swing emanates from the ground up, and the lower portions of the body—particularly the hips—play a major role. This bit of information should encourage players of smaller physical stature.

Since power comes from the lower half of the body, small players may find that they can easily perform the proper mechanics of a powerful swing. Small players are often quicker and have better balance than bigger players because their center of gravity is lower. Yes, this means that smaller players can also develop powerful swings.

Staying Closed

As mentioned in the previous chapter, a key part of the stealth stride is landing the front foot with the toe closed. In other words, the toe faces the plate, not toward the infield. It's not always possible to land with the toe perfectly closed, but it is the goal. This puts you in the best position to engage the movement of the big muscles of the legs and hips.

Even if the toe lands slightly open, it is okay. Concentrate on getting the toe perfectly closed. However, if the toe lands slightly open, you can still make a good swing. It's only when the toe points directly toward the pitcher that you've gotten yourself into a difficult position for making a good swing.

When the toe is closed, the body is also closed toward the

If you plant your stride foot with the toe open your shoulders and hips rotate open too soon.

pitcher; in other words, the hips and shoulders have not rotated and are still facing the plate. Why is this so important? If your toe is open, your front hip and shoulder will rotate open (toward the pitcher) too soon. In turn, this causes your hands to move forward prematurely, which reduces the acceleration of the bat when it meets the ball. This deceleration through the hitting zone reduces power.

Turning the hips is one of the keys to a powerful swing; it initiates the action of bringing the shoulders and upper body around. But if you turn the hips prematurely (before the heel of your stride foot hits the ground), you lose power in your swing. It also makes it more difficult to hit outside pitches. Here is what Wade Boggs said about the closed front toe: "You have to see what you're hitting. Striding with a closed toe enables you to keep your head in there a little longer." In other words, the closed toe prevents you from pulling your body and head away from the ball so that you can get a long look at the pitch. It also helps prevent all your weight from shifting too far forward when you stride.

When your toe lands closed, the hips and shoulders will also be closed; that is, they'll form a line pointing toward the pitcher, and the hands will stay back until you're ready to rotate the hips toward the pitcher. This means your body is square (hips and shoulders are facing the plate) at the moment your front foot lands and you have established a solid foundation from which to start the swing.

The hips definitely need to rotate to create bat speed and a powerful swing, but they should not turn too soon. That is why the closed toe is so important—because it temporarily restrains the movement of the hips. Ultimately, the energy from your hips and arms is applied to the ball in a powerful sequence starting with the rotation of the hips, thus generating maximum bat speed at contact.

As the hips rotate, the shoulders open and allow the hands and arms to drop down into the hitting zone (the hands don't move forward on their own). Explosive hips are your initial source of bat speed. When you come to separation (taking a stride forward and moving the bat back at the same time), most of your weight remains back till the stride foot plants (heel comes down). This is when you create a firm or stiff front leg, which allows your hips, torso, upper body, and shoulders to rotate. If your weight comes forward too soon, you lose that solid front side and the ability to quickly rotate—or explode—the hips.

Try this little exercise. From a balanced stance, stride forward and put all of your weight onto your front foot (your back foot should lift off the ground). With the weight totally on the front foot, your body now leans forward because your spine (and the bulk of your upper body) is centered over the front leg. If you now try to initiate a swing, that is, to rotate your hips, you have nothing to work against—no way to generate power.

In the correct swing the hip explosion rotates the back foot and shifts much of your weight onto a slightly bent front leg or against a stiff front leg. When the swing is made against a stiff front leg, it's called a "rotational" swing, and approximately 60 percent of your weight will remain on the ball of your back foot. Your back knee is at a 90-degree angle directly over the centerline of your body upon impact. Remember, while waiting for the pitch, concentrate on exploding your hips. If you explode your hips, your hands, head, and stiff (or slightly bent) front leg will all take care of themselves. Perhaps better than anyone, Barry Bonds exemplifies the hip explosion and all the elements necessary to make it happen. Watch him closely when he bats (if they pitch to him).

TRY TO SEE THE BALL HIT THE BAT

Every young player has probably heard this bit of advice: keep your eyes on the ball. In more accurate terms, he is being told to follow the pitch all the way with his eyes, even to the point of seeing the seams on the ball. Once again, this can only be done if your stride foot lands with toe closed. If not, your head and eyes will turn away and you will have trouble keeping your eyes on the ball.

Try to see the ball meet the bat, but don't get frustrated if you can't. Scientists don't agree on whether a batter can totally track a ball and actually see it collide with the bat. Some scientists say that, in fact, players lose the ball anywhere from five to twenty feet in front of them and rely on peripheral vision and kinesthetic feel, or muscle memory, to make contact.

Scientists do agree, however, that ideal tracking of a pitched ball requires minimal movement of the head. Studies show that excessive head movement throws off the balancing system and makes it much more difficult to track a ball. It's a good idea to not only keep your eyes on the ball but also to keep your head as still as possible.

Tennis legend Billie Jean King, when asked if she actually saw the tennis ball (traveling at a speed of 100 miles per hour or more) collide with her racket, said, "Sometimes I see it, sometimes I don't. When I do, I also see the spin of the ball." Wow, what vision. No wonder she was such a great champion!

Scientists know that the eyes lead the hands in what is known as eye-hand coordination. In other words, your eyes and brain calculate the location of the ball as it enters the hitting zone (that final stage of eye tracking). At that point some combination of direct vision,

The head stays as still or quiet as possible and moves slightly down and forward while the eyes track the ball.

peripheral vision, and muscle memory delivers the bat head to the ball. You can develop this coordination through repetition.

Although you may not be able to see the ball make contact with the bat, make it your goal anyway. It will help you keep your eyes focused on the ball from the time the pitcher releases it. Andre Dawson said, "I like to see the ball hit my bat. It's not going to happen every at-bat during the season, but I try to remain conscious of that and come close to it."

At the start of the swing, the chin should be near the front shoulder. Try to keep your head still as your body rotates through the swing. At the end of your swing, your head should be near your back shoulder. Avoid excessive head movement; the head should move *slightly* forward and downward during the stride but remain as still as possible during the hip rotation and the final split seconds of tracking the ball. Don't lift your head up too soon after making contact. Youngsters are anxious to see where the ball is going. Good hitters track the ball longer with their eyes than poor hitters do.

If you put your weight totally on the front foot you have no way to generate a powerful swing.

Drill

This drill promotes hip explosion. Place a ball on a tee. Get in a balanced stance. Move to separation (stride forward and bat back, with 60 to 70 percent of your weight back). Then check to make sure everything to this point is in position. Now you're ready to hit. Rotate your back hip forward (toward the pitcher) to move your hands to the ball;

Examples of correct hip rotation and leg action.

don't use your hands only. In other words, let your hip rotation and the opening of your shoulders bring your hands forward and down, left hand pulling and right hand pushing the barrel toward the contact point. This puts your body in perfect position to have the bat strike the ball.

Follow these steps:

1. Get to separation.
2. Check down, pausing for two counts.
3. Swing, using your hips.
4. Hit the ball up the middle.
5. Repeat steps 1 through 3.

Rotate your hips to move your hands to the ball; don't rely solely on the hands.

COACH'S BOX Steve Braun Says . . .

Stride with the front toe closed.

One of the biggest mistakes young hitters make is striding with the front toe open. This is common among players who stride and swing at the same time. The open toe causes them to rotate their hips and front side too soon, robbing them of power. The toe should be at least 45 degrees closed when the front foot lands. The more it is closed the better. A position of 100 percent closed would be when the foot is perpendicular to an imaginary line drawn between you and the pitcher. The closed toe allows the stride leg to stiffen with a slight angle or straighten completely, which then allows the hips to turn more powerfully.

You can't support a vigorous hip rotation without having your toe closed to a sufficient degree. Once you get the front toe closed and front leg locked, you then pivot on the back foot and rotate the back hip forward, that is, counterclockwise for a right-handed batter. This opens the front side (as opposed to the front toe opening up and prematurely clearing out the front side) and allows the hands to travel

The open toe is common among players who stride and swing at the same time.

The toe should be at least 45 degrees closed when the stride foot plants.

close to the torso and the barrel to accelerate through the hitting zone.

If a player has difficulty accomplishing this, I recommend soft toss or tee drills that require him to totally close his toes to make sure he is hitting against a firm front leg. Ask the player to set up in the box at a distance slightly farther away from the plate than normal and to take his stride toward the plate instead of toward the pitcher. This should force his toe to stay closed when his foot lands, giving him a sense of what the correct position of the front toe should look and feel like after it lands.

Or you can try the "heel up and heel down" drill. It is basically an imitation of what the Red Sox's Nomar Garciaparra does at the plate. Nomar takes a little wider stance, placing his stride foot where it would land if he took a normal stride. Then, instead of striding, he simply lifts the heel of his front foot (with toe already closed) and drops it back down again as he swings. By doing this, the player should be able to feel the strong support from the front leg that allows the hips to rotate and generate power.

Play It Again, Sam

- A powerful swing emanates from the lower body—mainly from the hips.
- Your stride foot should land with toe closed. This keeps your hips closed until the moment they explode open, producing maximum bat speed.
- Your hip rotation brings your hands forward; your hands do not move forward on their own.
- As your hips open, your front leg stiffens, creating a solid front side to explode against.
- If your hips turn too soon, (1) your head pulls away from the ball, reducing vision and making it more difficult to hit outside pitches; and (2) your hands move forward too soon, diminishing bat speed.
- Your hip explosion rotates your back foot so that in a fully rotational swing as much as 60 percent of your weight is on the ball of your back foot. Your back knee is at a 90-degree angle and directly over the centerline of your body upon impact.
- Keep your eyes focused on the ball and try to see it hit the bat.

7

DOWN AND UP

The Barrel Must Go Down
Before It Goes Up

> *Balls hit into the air are useless to personal and team production 90 percent of the time. It is skillful hitting to be a line drive/ground ball hitter.*
>
> —Mike Schmidt

Most of what we've learned to this point has focused on the movements of the lower body. However, once the hips begin to rotate and start their explosion, the hands assume a leading role. At this stage, the hands start forward and down into the hitting zone. Forward and down is best because it represents the shortest distance to the ball. Since a straight line is the shortest distance between two points, think of your bat barrel as point A and the ball as point B. First, point the knob of the bat at the ball. Then, fire the barrel directly at the ball. Bringing the hands forward and down keeps the swing short and compact and reduces the chance for error in the swing.

As you bring the hands and barrel down, keep the back elbow close to the body so the bat travels in a tight circle. After the initial downward move, get the barrel on the same plane or level as the pitch. Keep the barrel on plane and accelerate through impact. The correct swing starts down, then stays level (on the same plane as the pitch), and then goes up into a high follow-through with good extension.

Legendary hitting guru Charley Lau taught that the key to producing a level swing was to start the hands above the path of the ball's flight, bring them down and then forward, propelling the barrel of the bat along the path or plane of the pitch. He even allowed that "a tendency toward a slight uppercut [through the impact

The correct swing starts down and levels off on the plane of the pitch.

zone] isn't all that bad, as long as it remains slight. The problems occur when the uppercut is an extreme loop."

As a hitter, think "down, level, and long." You should think "long" because the swing should reach full extension before it finishes. The more level your swing, the larger the area where contact can be made squarely. Obviously, the entire swing is not level, but it must be level in the middle of the swing plane and through the contact zone. The arms finish the swing by taking the bat into a high follow-through.

77

The correct swing finishes with a high follow-through.

Ted Williams said, "A level swing is the shortest possible stroke. It gives you more time to wait, to keep from getting fooled." An examination of a fastball's trajectory from the point it leaves the pitcher's hand to the arrival at home plate confirms the value of a level swing that gets on the same plane as the pitch.

Here is a little physics of baseball to help you understand what's happening when someone hurls that next fastball your way: All fastballs travel a downward path because (1) the pitcher is standing on a raised mound, and (2) gravity pulls pitches toward the ground. Even though all pitched balls travel from high to low, some—when thrown at speeds of 90 miles per hour or more, do not drop as much. To many batters, these pitches appear to rise, but—because of the laws of physics—they don't. Scientists have shown that these higher-speed pitches just don't drop as much. Batters, who are used to the trajectory of slower-moving pitches, simply swing under them and understandably exclaim, "His fastball has hop to it" or "He's got a rising fastball." A level swing or a swing that travels directly along the slightly descending path of a pitch produces the best contact. It puts the barrel on a direct collision course with the ball. Even if the swing is a little early or late, you can still make good contact with this swing.

78

Flawed Swings

Several things can go wrong on the way to a perfect swing. Here are four flaws to avoid: the loop, the uppercut, the cast, and the chop.

The Loop

A looping swing takes your hands and bat on a longer route to the ball. Looping swings include moving the hands out toward the plate (away from your rotating spine) and then forward, or moving them back, down, and then up, which is commonly referred to as a "hitch." Any time your hands don't initially move down and forward you've got a loop in your swing. This indirect path to the ball will hurt your chances of making solid contact. Here are a few nasty problems presented by a looping swing:

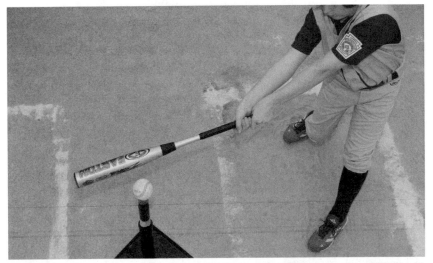

Compare the way the swing in the first photo has disconnected—that is, moved away from the body, its power source—with the swing in the second photo, which shows the hands staying closer to the rotating hips. This enables them to speed the barrel through the hitting zone.

- It takes longer for a looping swing to reach the ball; therefore, you must start the swing earlier. In turn, this gives you less time to decide whether or not to swing.
- When your arms move away from your body, you slow down the swing and make the bat feel heavier.
- If your arms or hands go back, down, and then up you have the early makings of an uppercut stroke (see following), which creates more misses (swinging strikes) and mishits (fly balls and topspin grounders).

The Uppercut

Here is what an uppercut swing looks like: As the swing begins, the batter collapses his rear leg and opens his front hip prematurely. His weight tilts backward, causing his front shoulder to come up. The hands and bat naturally come down, which means they must go back up to hit the ball—and the uppercut is born.

In an uppercut swing the front shoulder comes up and the bat barrel approaches the ball from below.

The greater the uppercut, the less time your bat spends on the plane of the ball; therefore, the less likely it will be that you'll make square contact. As a result, if you make contact, you'll hit lots of fly balls and topspin ground balls. It also puts your body into a weak position at the point of contact, thus limiting your power. You also lose full arm extension and diminish your weight transfer.

The Cast

In fishing, the casting motion sweeps your hands and pole out and away from your body. It is the opposite of what a batter should do with his hands and bat. The cast extends your lead arm outward toward the plate instead of pulling (with the left hand) and pushing (with the right hand) the knob of the bat toward the pitch. Casting is also referred to as "hitting around the ball" or "getting your hands outside the ball."

Casting creates problems. It lengthens your swing, which means you need to start your swing earlier. You will likely hit the inside pitch off your fist, and you'll be more easily fooled by the off-speed pitch. Also, it reduces power because you cannot swing the bat as fast when it is so far from the center of your body (spine). Think of how a figure skater speeds up his spin—he keeps his hands close to his body. When you swing at a pitch you need to keep your hands close to your body so you can rotate your hips quickly and then fire the hands through the impact zone. If they're floating out and away from the body, you cannot generate the necessary hand and bat speed.

The Chop

Sometimes a coach will instruct a youngster to swing down on the ball. This is often misinterpreted and taken literally. While it is true that the initial movement of the hands and bat is forward and down, the bat must level off well before it nears the point of contact. The bat stays level through the ball and then rises to a high follow-through. Simply a chop (without the leveling off and high follow-through) will rarely produce square contact with the ball, resulting mostly in weak ground balls. Similar to an upper-cut, the chop reduces the time the bat is on the same plane as the ball.

LEARN TO HIT LINE DRIVES

Coaches sometimes pose this question to their young players: What is the definition of a fly ball? The answer, of course, is "an out." Mike Schmidt didn't learn the secret to his personal hitting success until he realized the importance of the level swing. From that point, Schmidt's career took off. He discovered the level swing is the remedy for the dreaded fly ball disease.

Ground balls and line drives are the most productive ways to hit. In fact, managers prefer their players to hit ground balls rather than fly balls. Here's an interesting way to look at it. If a pitcher coaxes every hitter in the lineup to hit a fly ball, he has a good chance of pitching a no-hitter. But if every batter hits a ground ball, at least a few runs will likely score. This is because ground balls have a chance to go through the infield for a base hit. At the very least, ground balls force the infielders to make successful catches and throws. Line drives are even better because they are difficult to catch and often land in a gap. In contrast, fly balls are very catchable. As you can see, the odds are clearly on the side of the batter who hits hard ground balls and line drives.

The player who uppercuts tries to hit the ball in the air by dropping his back shoulder before swinging. As a result, he usually hits under the ball and pops it up, or he hits the top of the ball and produces a weak ground ball. Also, a player who uses a heavy bat may experience the bat dropping below the hitting level, forcing him to pull the bat up into the zone. In this case, the player should either choose a lighter bat or choke up.

Uppercuts often have their roots in childhood Wiffle ball games. An upward swing seems to be an effective way to hit fly balls. No doubt, fly balls are more exciting at that stage than ground balls. Tee Ball also creates the need to lift the ball off the tee and into the outfield, resulting in an uppercut. This can be a tough habit to break by the time the player reaches Little League age. Whether it's Wiffle ball or Tee Ball, it's best to swing "down, level, and long"—that is, bring the hands down, swing the bat level, and finish the swing long (with the arms extended just at or beyond impact). This swing pattern will get the results you want and the mechanics you need to excel.

Drill

This simple drill is designed to commit the forward and down motion of the hands to muscle memory. The drill requires another person to throw soft tosses or the use of a batting tee. Select a short bat. Place only your bottom hand on the bat in a severely choked grip (eight or nine inches from the knob). Place your top hand on your right hip, thumb and forefinger facing forward. Take a balanced stance. As

Push your right hip and pull the head of the bat to the ball with your bottom hand.

the ball is tossed into the hitting zone, vigorously push your trailing hip (right hip for a right-handed batter) so that it opens quickly, and simultaneously pull your hand (and the choked bat) to the ball with a quick, downward motion. Continue the swing toward the pitcher after contact. Repeat. This gives you a quick, short, and direct swing to the ball and promotes the powerful hip action that is necessary for leading the hands into a swing.

COACH'S BOX Steve Braun Says . . .

Avoid making that uppercut swing.

The biggest mistake that I see young hitters make is trying to lift the ball in the air. It means they haven't learned how to start the swing correctly. The proper swing starts by pulling the bat down to the ball and forward. Some young players, however, tend to add a little loop at the beginning of the swing by first dropping the bat down and then swinging up at the ball.

84

Hitting off a batting tee may contribute to this problem. In an effort to miss the tee and hit only the ball, players get into bad mechanics. They drop the bat down and get it on plane with the ball too soon (in this instance, the plane would be parallel to the ground at the height of the tip of the batting tee). This allows them to lift the ball while avoiding contact with the rubber tip of the tee. Because of their fear of hitting the tee, they program an uppercut arc into their swing. By using a proper swing, however, the bottom of the barrel actually makes slight contact with the tee. In a proper approach to the ball on a tee, contact with the ball is made just as the downward arc is bottoming out and moving on plane.

Another factor contributing to this problem is the emphasis on the home run. Youngsters want to learn how to lift the ball in the air, thinking that home runs will result. Let's face it, home runs are fun

The proper swing produces contact with the ball and the top of the tee.

but not everyone is going to be a home run hitter. Young players might be able to get away with that long, looping swing against slow pitchers they face in their younger ages, but as they get older and the pitches come in at greater velocities, that long, looping, upper-cut swing will not work. In fact, only two things can happen, and they're both bad: (1) the pitch will be past you before you can get the barrel in its path, or (2) if you do make contact, the result will be a foul tip, lazy fly ball, or pop-up.

Play It Again, Sam

- Once the hips start to rotate, the hands start forward and down into the hitting zone, with the knob of the bat pointing at the ball.
- The correct swing starts down, then levels off (on the same plane as the ball) through the ball, and then rises to a high follow-through.
- A level swing creates a larger area where contact can be made squarely.
- Avoid these swing flaws: looping, uppercutting, casting, and chopping.
- Ground balls and line drives are the most productive ways to hit.

8

UP AND DOWN

Palm Up, Palm Down at Contact

> *The bottom hand acts as a guide to put the bat in position to use the top hand. Once this happens, the bat is thrown or pushed into the ball by the top hand.*
>
> —Richie Zisk

Perhaps the most interesting and informative action photo of any good hitter's swing is the one taken at the moment the bat meets the ball. So many important lessons can be learned from this single snapshot. If it is truly a good swing, the photo will depict many of the things we've discussed in previous chapters. For example, the front toe is closed (or slightly closed), the weight is centered on the middle of the body, the rear heel is lifted, the rear toe and knee are pointed to the ground, and the bat head is on the ball. In addition, the photo shows you the position of the hands at

At contact the hands are in a palm up, palm down position.

impact. The palm of the bottom hand is facing down to the ground and the palm of the top hand is facing up to the sky. This positioning of the hands puts the bat on a level plane at impact.

Hands into the Zone

As the body begins to rotate, the bottom hand pulls the bat into the hitting zone while the top hand pushes the bat toward the ball. At contact, the top hand is underneath the bat (palm up) so the bottom surface rests against the pads of your palm just below the fingers, providing extra support for the weight of the bat and firm control of the head of the bat. The forearm of the bottom hand is nearly perpendicular to the bat, with the palm of the bottom hand facing down. The top forearm moves in a way that simulates the swing of an ax. The head and eyes are fixed as well as possible on the point of contact. The palm up, palm down position occurs only in the area of impact. Trying to do it earlier in the swing disrupts the proper sequence of movements and dramatically reduces the speed of the swing.

As the bat moves into the hitting zone, your wrists remain firm and unbroken—just as if you were to hit a tree with an ax. When the hands are six to eight inches from the point of contact, the wrists snap the bat through the hitting zone. This is not the same as rolling the wrists (rolling your top hand over). The snap fires the barrel of the bat into the ball. This is a top hand maneuver. If the left hand and left side (of the right-handed hitter) dominate the swing, the snap will not occur. The right hand and right arm must guide the bat to provide the snap through the hitting zone. If you don't snap your wrists correctly, you will likely swing late at fastballs, have trouble handling inside pitches, and be regularly fooled by off-speed pitches because of the need to start your swing early.

The snap does not alter the path of the bat; however, rolling the wrists at impact will change its course by lifting the bat over the top of the ball. This often results in whiffs or weak ground balls. It does not produce power. Rather, it disrupts the accuracy and mechanics of your swing. Therefore, do not roll your wrists at impact.

As the hips open farther, it causes the shoulders to open. Your hands and arms are well out in front of the plate, with your bat trailing slightly behind. Again, think of swinging an ax at the side of a tree trunk. Your wrists must be firm when the ax strikes the tree. Similarly, your wrists must be solid as they enter the hitting zone. Hit the ball in front of the plate.

Ted Williams described the swing as a hard push-swing. The top hand pushes and the bottom hand pulls. Since you can push harder than you can pull, the top hand generates the most force. You push hard through the impact area. The top hand snaps forward as it push-swings through the zone.

LOWER THE BODY, IMPROVE THE SWING

When you picture a level swing, you probably imagine the bat making contact with a pitch that is belt-high. But how is it possible to get the bat on a level plane when swinging at a low strike, about knee-high? That is an important question because pitchers are taught from an early age to keep the ball low; therefore, it pays to learn to hit the low pitch squarely.

The legs are the answer to hitting the low pitch. The hitter needs to become shorter (lower his body) in order to get his hands and eyes down to a position where he can swing the bat on a level plane. The lazy and ineffective method of hitting the low pitch is by simply dropping the barrel of the bat to the ball, without lowering the body. This makes it more difficult to make square contact with any regularity because the bat is at an angle closer to being perpendicular to the ground, which significantly reduces the amount of hitting surface available. As a result of this narrow hitting surface, the batter is more likely to swing through the ball, pop it up (if the swing is a little too early), or hammer it into the ground (if the swing is a little too late). And even if he were to hit it on the sweet spot, the angle of his swing may result in a hook or slice, which reduces distance. In contrast, a bat that approaches the ball on a level plane provides the maximum amount of surface on which to hit the ball squarely.

Lower your center of gravity by flexing your legs to hit the low pitch but keep everything else about your swing the same.

So, how do you get down to hit that low strike? After your stride foot has fully landed and your hip rotation has started, flex your legs as if you are sitting down. You're simply lowering your center of gravity; everything else about your swing remains the same. The difference is that your bat will approach the ball on a level plane, with your eyes closer to the ball.

Drill

Place the ball on a tee. Establish a balanced stance with the ball opposite your stride foot. Slowly pull the bat down to the ball and extend your arms and hands into the palm up, palm down position. Make sure your right elbow is folded down and in to your right side (for right-handed hitters), then extend it as you move the bat to the contact point. Keep your head locked and your eyes on

Tuck your right elbow into your right side as you move toward contact, hands palm up, palm down.

the bat in the impact area. See and feel the position of your hands—top hand up, bottom hand down. Repeat this slowly 10 times until you sense the correct palm positions. The goal is for the hands to automatically (through muscle memory) arrive at the ball in the palm up, palm down position.

An abbreviated version of this drill is to place a ball on a tee and assume the point of contact. Then check the hands for proper positioning.

COACH'S BOX Steve Braun Says . . .

When tracking the pitch, try to see the ball hit the bat.

When I was a young player, my father gave me some very valuable advice: "See the ball hit the bat!"

It was his way of telling me to watch the ball from the moment it leaves the pitcher's hand to the moment it hits my bat. This is very helpful in developing hand-eye coordination and promoting good hitting habits. For example, it keeps your front shoulder closed, prevents your head from pulling out too early, and enables you to distinguish the type of spin on the ball that identifies the pitch. When a batter tries to see the ball hit the bat, he can avoid swinging too early at breaking balls. This is because he is able to wait and let the ball get deeper into the hitting zone, which gives him more time to determine whether it is a ball or strike.

Here is how to focus your eyes properly when tracking a pitch: First, keep them looking slightly up toward the pitcher during the windup and until he reaches the release point in his motion. After release, drop your eyes slightly toward the hitting area and then stop to focus as the ball moves into the hitting zone.

As the back shoulder comes around to replace the front shoulder, allow your head to rise up naturally.

Here is a verbal drill to use during practice. It will reinforce your focusing on the pitch. As you swing at the pitch, say out loud, "See the ball hit the bat!" This will help you to concentrate on what you're trying to accomplish with each swing—that is, see the ball hit the bat. By saying this aloud, you'll remind yourself to lock your eyes into the correct position. Remember: keep your head from moving and your eyes will focus properly. When you practice this drill you will be amazed at how long your eyes and head stay in the correct position.

Do not consciously think about keeping your head down after contact. Some players give too much thought to keeping their chin on the front shoulder and head down all the way to the end of the follow-through. If the head is not released soon after contact, it can actually restrict bat speed and impede the follow-through. As the back shoulder comes around to replace the position of the front shoulder, allow your head to rise up naturally and your eyes to pick up the flight of the ball. This will allow the arms to complete a balanced follow-through.

Play It Again, Sam

- At the moment of impact, when the ball meets the bat, the palm of the bottom hand faces down to the ground and the palm of the top hand faces up to the sky. This puts the bat on a level plane.
- The bottom hand pulls the bat into the hitting zone, and the top hand pushes the bat toward the ball.
- The wrists are firm and solid as the hands bring the bat down into the hitting zone.

- When the hands are six to eight inches from the point of contact, the wrists snap the bat through the hitting zone. The top hand initiates this wrist snap, but it is not the same as rolling the wrists.
- To hit a low strike you need to go down and get it—that is, flex your legs as if you are sitting down. This allows the bat to approach the ball on a level plane, thus making available the maximum amount of hitting surface.

9

THE MARK McGWIRE MOVE

Finish High, Finish Long

> *If you don't follow through, everything you've done up to that point will be wasted.*
>
> —Charley Lau

In Chapter 7 you learned to visualize the arc of the swing as "down, level, and long." The first stage is down; then it levels off for a brief distance. The last phase is *long*—when you keep the bat on the same plane as the pitch, the arms fully extend, and the bat finishes high after contact. The correct throwing motion is similar. A pitcher does not stop his arm at the release point; he follows through to produce maximum velocity and a consistent arm angle. The same applies to hitting. The batter should hit through the ball and finish the swing. At impact, the bat's momentum can slow down if you don't follow through with force and purpose.

Some young players are afraid of getting their hands stung when the bat meets the ball. If a player lacks sufficient strength, the force of the incoming ball can be greater than the speed of the bat, thus causing the bat to rebound or vibrate when contact is made. This resistance can be intimidating, and players often respond by slowing down the swing as the bat approaches the ball and nearly stopping the swing. This deceleration halts the movement of the body through the swing, thus reducing power and distance. This problem can be corrected, however, once the player begins to experience the results of swinging through the ball. He'll notice the ball going much farther and with greater force. Remember: hit through the ball, not to the ball.

Extended and High

It is important to keep the arms moving toward full extension after contact and into the follow-through, creating a large arc. Finishing high helps to maintain extension. A short follow-through often results when the arm of the top hand folds over the arm of the bottom hand too soon. This causes the arm of the bottom hand to fold at the elbow, reducing the arc of the swing and slowing bat speed. Keep this descriptive phrase in mind: short to the ball and long through it. "Short" refers to pulling the hands down quickly in a short, direct path to the ball at the beginning of the swing; and long refers to continuing the arms and bat toward the pitcher after contact, with full arm extension. In the words of Dusty Baker, "You want to start your swing short and finish long—in other words, extension."

Both arms should reach full extension at impact or just beyond impact, forming a triangle with the shoulders. Be careful not to arrive at full arm extension before contact, or you risk not hitting the ball squarely. With arms fully extended, the bat circles your body almost completely and finishes high and behind you. If you make a

Keep the arms moving toward full extension contact.

well-balanced swing from start to finish, you'll be in a balanced position from which to start running to first base. If you make a poorly executed swing, you'll know it. A well-balanced finish feels good and is a sign that the earlier parts of the swing were also good.

The arms reach full extension at impact or just beyond impact, when they briefly form a triangle with the shoulders.

When finishing high, release your top hand from the bat at the point where your arm extension would be restricted if you had held on to the bat. On most pitches, that occurs well after making contact with the ball. Note: it is not necessarily wrong to hold onto the bat with both hands when finishing the swing; however, this is more commonly applied when making a fully rotational swing or when the hands must be pulled in to hit an inside pitch.

When releasing the top hand during your swing, never let it feel like you are swinging with only one hand. If that occurs, you are releasing your hand too soon. During Mark McGwires's chase to break Roger Maris's home run record in 1998, McGwire's home run swing was shown everywhere. The snapshot of his completed swing displayed his classic one-handed, high follow-through—at its apex it looks like he's holding a torch at the top.

Merv Rettenmund, Detroit Tigers hitting coach, said, "The biggest change in recent years is the high follow-through. When you hit the ball hard with the high follow-through, it's going to go out." Finishing high also helps to keep your head down, which produces a stronger follow-through. Your chin should be on your back shoulder at the end of your swing. As mentioned in the previous chapter, do not roll your wrists because it restricts the extension of your bottom arm.

SWING LEVEL TO GET ADDED DISTANCE

Research has been conducted on the effect of backspin on a batted ball. The results indicate that backspin significantly improves the lift and carry of the ball. In other words, a ball hit with backspin will stay aloft longer and travel farther, helping it to reach the gaps and fences faster and more frequently. The more backspin, the better. Applying a level swing to the ball just below the ball's centerline, or equator, creates backspin. In contrast, hitting the ball with an uppercut creates topspin, which reduces distance because the topspin causes the ball to sink as it travels in the air. Swinging down to the ball and creating backspin is what caused Mike Schmidt's career to take off. He stopped trying to hit home runs with an upward swing and concentrated on hitting hard line drives with a level swing and backspin.

Creation of backspin starts from the point of contact where the palm of the top hand should be facing up and the palm of the bottom hand should be facing down. The top hand pushes the bat through the impact zone and into the finish. This pushing motion and contact with the ball on a level plane is what creates line drives with backspin. Another important ingredient to producing backspin and distance is the high finish. Two hands are on the bat upon impact.

101

Once contact has been made, the top hand pushes the bat forward through the ball. However, at that point, the top hand comes off the bat, allowing the bottom hand to let the bat go forward, up, and out. This extension maximizes the distance on the ball and finishes your swing. Keeping both hands on the bat after impact causes a roll of the wrists that creates topspin, which will cause balls to sink and potential home runs to fall short. Keeping both hands on the bat also shortens the length of the swing. Hitting through the ball requires good arm and bat extension that carries through into a high finish.

Drill

This drill can be done alone in a batting cage or in an open area. Neither a ball nor a tee is required—only a Wiffle ball bat.

Establish a balanced stance and then take a swing at an imaginary pitch in the middle of the strike zone. Start your swing by pulling the bat down to the ball. Fully extend your arms at or just beyond the contact point. Shortly after contact is made, release the bat from both hands. Keep your arms extended after release and carry them into a high finish. If the bat is released at the correct time, it will go straight forward—not down at the ground. This drill teaches the timing required to release the top hand.

COACH'S BOX Steve Braun Says . . .

Continue the level part of the swing after contact.

Finishing the swing high into the follow-through is important, but it must follow good arm extension. In other words, be careful not to raise the bat too soon when moving through the contact zone. If you do, you will come out of the swing before completing full extension. Continue the level part of the swing after contact and extend the bat toward the pitcher before moving it up and around behind your front shoulder. The end of the bat should momentarily point to the pitcher during this extension phase.

If you don't create a flat extension a lot of bad things can happen: (1) you shorten the impact zone, (2) you come out of the swing too soon, (3) you cut off the swing, and (4) you do not extend the arms. Without this flat extension you make poor contact and lose power. Remember that you must keep the bat flat (and swinging along a plane that intercepts the flight of the ball) before letting it rise and come around your body.

In my experience as a hitting instructor I have found that players have more difficulty with getting their arms fully extended than they do with achieving a high finish. Players who have a steep swing— that is, they chop down—have the most trouble. They stay steep too long. To improve, they need to concentrate on getting the bat level during the hitting zone. If they don't, they'll hit the ball into the ground because their swing never moves out of the downward path into the level phase of the swing. To correct this, you should concentrate on swinging the bat level or near level while in the flat extension phase, and then follow this with a high finish.

Continue the level part of the swing after contact and extend the bat toward the pitcher.

Play It Again, Sam

- The last phase of the swing is full extension of the arms and bat as they hit through the ball, followed by a high finish.
- Don't reduce the speed of the bat before, during, or after contact. It stops the movement of your body and reduces power and distance. Hit through the ball, not to the ball.
- Both arms should reach full arm extension at impact or just beyond impact, forming a triangle with the shoulders.
- Finish high by releasing the top hand from the bat shortly after making contact with the ball.
- Backspin makes the ball carry longer, reaching the gaps and fences. Create backspin by pushing the bat into the ball on a level plane, striking the ball just below its centerline, and then finishing high.

10

ROCK, WIGGLE, AND ROLL

Lower the Tension, Powder the Ball

> *You must develop your own method for getting comfortable at the plate.*
> —Joe Morgan

The previous chapters have addressed key ingredients of the swing—from the grip to the follow-through. However, one other essential element remains: relaxation. Think of a chef who prepares a special entrée by following a recipe to perfection, and then adds that final, extra touch—perhaps a pinch of this or that. In the case of the swing, that extra ingredient is relaxation. Without it, the chance of executing a perfect swing is diminished.

Hitting is similar to dancing. A dancer's movements must be fluid and tension-free. The movements, balance, and flexibility all stem from the core of the body. The same theory applies to the swing. It's a proven fact that muscles react more quickly and accurately when they're in a relaxed state. If a batter understands how tension can destroy a potentially good swing, then why let tension take over? This can be a struggle for some players. Slow, rhythmical movements and relaxed hands in the loading stage put you in the best position to hit the ball with maximum results.

Look at a variety of major league hitters and you'll see different ways of staying loose and getting into a good position to hit. Their body movements enable them to stay relaxed and move through the ball as a whole body, not just hands and legs. You've never seen a good dancer without rhythm, and you've never seen a good hitter without rhythm.

As mentioned in Chapter 1, tension is the enemy. Once it gains a hold on you, it spreads throughout your body and even your mind. It restricts your movements and prevents you from making flowing and graceful swings with full extension of your arms and bat. Instead, your swing becomes mechanical and stiff. Tension also reduces bat speed, power, flexibility, and whip action. Moreover, tension negatively affects your mind's performance, which is vital because of the critical interaction of mind and body in the swing.

What are some telltale signs of tension in a batter?

- *Death grip on the bat.* This is the white-knuckle syndrome. You can almost see the tension travel from the hands through the rest of the body. It can nearly immobilize a batter. You're going to need all the strength and reaction speed you can muster once you begin to swing, so don't waste any valuable energy choking the bat handle while waiting for the pitch. Liken it to a flashlight battery that loses power when you leave it on accidentally. The next time you use it, the power of the beam won't be as bright. Hold the bat loosely while waiting for the delivery. Don't worry; your muscles and grip will automatically tighten when the bat moves toward the ball.

- *Locked, stiff knees.* This reduces the flexibility in the lower body. Remember, your power comes from the hips and legs. Tension prevents them from performing their important role to the maximum extent.
- *Happy feet.* Hitters who repeatedly move their feet display their tension and lack of confidence to everyone in the ballpark. The

White knuckles are a sign of tension.

first person to notice is the pitcher, who immediately gains the advantage in terms of confidence. He knows an easy out when he sees one. The batter's balance, weight shift, timing, and power are also jeopardized.

107

What can a player do to reduce tension?

- Slowly and rhythmically move your body forward and backward to release tension and promote relaxation. Players who have rhythmical movement in their bodies are the least likely to have tension. In contrast, a player who stands like a statue in a park is probably tense from head to foot. However, too much movement can be counterproductive, so just make slow and easy movements that don't disrupt balance and timing.
- Step out of the batter's box and take a couple of deep breaths to let tension flow progressively out of the body—one body part at a time.
- Stand up straight and let your body go limp and then shake from your shoulders and arms.

Make short or long waggles to keep your body relaxed and tension-free.

- Make short waggles of the bat forward and back between your feet (à la Mark McGwire) or longer ones. This keeps your hands and wrists loose and your body relaxed.
- Open and close the fingers of one hand and then the other hand while waiting for the delivery of the pitch. This repeated regripping (or milking the bat) prevents the hands from forming a lengthy death grip.
- Don't think about hitting a home run; it only creates unnecessary tension. Try to hit to all fields—hit the ball where it's pitched. For example, if the ball is on the outside part of the plate, hit it to the opposite field.
- Shorten your swing for more control and confidence. You'll make contact more often.
- Don't be afraid to fail. Fear tightens your muscles. Be confident by trusting your swing.

- Know your capabilities as a ballplayer and don't try to be someone you're not. It will only result in frustration from failing to play up to lofty and unrealistic expectations, and your confidence will be deflated. Set realistic goals for yourself, but be careful not to set the bar too low.

RELAXATION CAN LEAD TO CONFIDENCE

Confidence is a word mentioned often as being vital to success in any area of life, including baseball. But how does one acquire confidence? Ironically, it is sometimes the product of success, in which case the challenge becomes maintaining the confidence. More often, however, confidence is gained before success arrives, and confidence becomes the reason for success. In the case of hitting, relaxation can lead to confidence—as long as other factors do not undermine the effort. As in most endeavors (for example golf, public speaking, test taking), the more relaxed you are, the more productive you will be. Consider a student who is about to take an exam. If he enters the exam in a relaxed, confident state of mind, he will likely perform much better than if he is tense and fearful. Tension freezes the mind, making it difficult to process information effectively or recall facts and figures readily.

A batter always needs to display an air of confidence. It starts in the dugout and follows him to the on-deck circle and finally into the batter's box. It isn't cockiness; it's a quiet confidence—a feeling that is expressed in the way you walk and your loose, relaxed movements (body language). The intent is not only to let the pitcher and opposing players detect your confidence, but also to make it a permanent impression in your own mind that you are aware of at all times.

You've seen confident people in all walks of life. As soon as they walk into a room, their confidence is recognizable. It's the same way with a batter who walks to the plate and takes his stance. He looks like he belongs there, confident in his ability to powder the ball—he has no doubt or fear. And others know it too.

Drill

This drill requires only a bat, ball, and pitcher. Establish a balanced stance. With weight on your front foot, hold the bat with both hands and point it straight at the pitcher. From this position, bring the bat back slowly in a low arc along with your body. Keep your hands and arms loose throughout the movement. Once back in the loaded position, swing. Do this once without a pitch thrown. Then repeat the process and swing the second time. This teaches rhythm and relaxation.

110

COACH'S BOX Steve Braun Says . . .

Play pepper to improve the start of your swing.

The swing breaks down into three distinct parts: start, bottom, and finish. The start of the swing is a downward and forward action of the hands toward the ball. At the start or early part of the swing your hands should be above the ball. To do this you should start down to meet the ball.

During the second part of the swing—where it bottoms out or flattens out for a short distance, perhaps an inch or two—contact is made with the ball. In the third part, the swing moves upward at a very slight angle, perhaps 4 to 5 degrees, into the follow-through.

I believe that hitters should concentrate primarily on part one of the swing because if you start the swing properly, the next two parts should happen automatically. In fact, thinking about the last two parts and the need to get the bat moving slightly upward at the end of the swing may cause an uppercut. The batter will start his swing incorrectly by dropping his hands to a point lower than the path of the ball and will then adjust to meet the ball by swinging up. It is best to learn part one sufficiently because a poorly executed part one creates problems with parts two and three.

The hand action in the first eight inches of the swing is the key to the swing. You actually pull the bat down and forward with your bottom hand, pointing the knob of the bat at the ball. I was trying to explain this motion to a youngster once and he asked me, "Do you mean you want me to swing on a *slant*?"

That terminology made sense to him and it's an accurate description. I've even used slanted or angled support cables in batting cages to help reinforce this part of the swing motion. Players would stand next to the cables and run their hands or bat down and along the direction of the cable to feel the motion of pulling forward and down.

111

During this action the hands must start inside the flight or path of the ball. In other words, they must be fairly close to the body, perhaps six to eight inches.

Pepper is a hit-and-catch game that can be played by two or more players. One player bats the ball—grounders or line drives—to the fielder or fielders who stand approximately 20 to 25 feet away, fielding and soft tossing pitches to the batter. Unfortunately, pepper is seldom played today, especially among youngsters, who may never have been taught the game. However, pepper is still very helpful because it requires the hitter to pull the bat down and forward in order to hit grounders and line drives, and it teaches the batter how

Pepper is a hit-and-catch game that can be played with two or more players. It teaches bat control by requiring the batter to hit the ball in different directions.

112

to hit the ball in different directions (pull, straight, and to opposite field) by creating different angles of contact with the barrel of the bat. As a major leaguer, I played pepper before games to warm up. It improved my bat control and ability to hit to all fields. And it helped me to keep my hands up high enough to start down on pitches, even the high pitch. Try it. It can do the same for you.

Play It Again, Sam

- Relaxation is the final ingredient that produces a perfect swing. Tension is the enemy.
- You've never seen a good dancer without rhythm, and you've never seen a good hitter without rhythm.

- Telltale signs of tension are a death grip; locked, stiff knees; and happy feet.
- Do the following to reduce tension: make slow and rhythmical movements forward and backward; waggle the bat; take a few deep breaths; open and close the fingers of your hands (milk the bat); don't think about hitting home runs; don't be afraid to fail; and don't try to do too much.
- Relaxation leads to confidence. Look and feel confident at the plate so others recognize it (especially the pitcher).

113

Appendix

What's Your Hitting Quotient?

A Grading System of Baseball Hitting Skills

Now at bat _____ Age _____

Bats: Left _____   Right _____   Height _____   Weight _____

Part 1: Basic Setup

Score two points for each correct position.

		Points
1.	Balanced: stable when pushed at sternum	0–2
2.	Feet slightly more than shoulder-width apart	0–2
3.	Knees flexed, upper body slightly bent at waist	0–2
4.	Head/both eyes turned toward pitcher, eyes level	0–2
5.	Hands above top of strike zone	0–2

Total: _____ *of 10*

Part 2: Through Swing and Follow-Through

Score one point for each skill demonstrated correctly.

Points

1. Hands and stride foot separate—hands move
   back as stride foot moves forward as 60 percent
   of weight stays over spine or rear hip; hands not
   carried forward with step of stride foot   0–1
2. Stride is short (four to six inches),
   no overstriding   0–1
3. Position of stride foot is closed,
   perpendicular to pitcher   0–1
4. First move of hands to ball is down, left hand
   pulling/right hand pushing with knob leading
   toward ball at start of downward movement   0–1
5. Route to ball stays inside: no dropping,
   no sweeping, no circling or going around
   path of ball with hands   0–1
6. As hips rotate, head aligns over spine or
   near rear hip   0–1
7. Hip rotation leads hands and arms into
   hitting zone   0–1
8. Spine angle doesn't move past perpendicular   0–1
9. Hands reach impact palm up/palm down;
   doesn't prematurely roll the top hand over
   or shorten swing arc   0–1
10. Arms move briefly through triangle position
    just after contact   0–1

Total: _____ of 10

Part 3: Live Batting Skills

Set up a station where you throw pitches at batting-practice speed to the batter. Test for the player's ball-strike recognition, eye-hand coordination, and quality at-bat.

A. Ball-Strike Recognition

Throw five pitches. Score four points for each correct call by batter who observes and calls out "ball" or "strike" but does not swing at each pitch.

	Points
Pitch 1	0–4
Pitch 2	0–4
Pitch 3	0–4
Pitch 4	0–4
Pitch 5	0–4

Total: _____ of 20

B. Eye-Hand Coordination

Throw 10 pitches and score each pitch the batter attempts to hit. Use the same 10 pitches to score the batter's eye-hand coordination and his quality at-bat (section C). Score one point each time the batter successfully makes contact with the ball. Score any contact of the bat and ball—including foul tips—as a point.

	Points
Pitch 1	0–1
Pitch 2	0–1
Pitch 3	0–1
Pitch 4	0–1
Pitch 5	0–1
Pitch 6	0–1

Pitch 7	0–1
Pitch 8	0–1
Pitch 9	0–1
Pitch 10	0–1

Total: _____ *of 10*

C. Quality At-Bat

Throw 10 pitches at which the batter offers. Use the same 10 pitches to score the batter's quality at-bat and his eye-hand coordination (section B). Classify the attempts to hit the ball or actual hits as follows:

1. Miss (M), which is a swinging strike and is scored as a zero (0).
2. Line Drive (LD), which is graded from 7 to 10, depending on its quality (force, carry, conformation to or deviation from "frozen rope" trajectory).
3. Fly Ball (FB), which is graded from 0 to 7, depending on its quality (a pop-up is a 0 but a ball hit hard and long in the air, such as an outfield "gap" hit or a fly ball that would carry over the outfielders, would be a 7).
4. Ground Ball (GB), which would be graded from 0 to 7, depending on its quality (a topped high hopper would be a 0 while a sizzling-hot, fast-skipping ground ball would be a 7). Use common sense and discretion but reward balls that are struck solidly.

118

	(Circle one and rate)				*Points*
Pitch 1	M (0)	LD (7–10)	FB (0–7)	GB (0–7)	_____
Pitch 2	M (0)	LD (7–10)	FB (0–7)	GB (0–7)	_____
Pitch 3	M (0)	LD (7–10)	FB (0–7)	GB (0–7)	_____
Pitch 4	M (0)	LD (7–10)	FB (0–7)	GB (0–7)	_____
Pitch 5	M (0)	LD (7–10)	FB (0–7)	GB (0–7)	_____

Pitch 6	M (0)	LD (7–10)	FB (0–7)	GB (0–7)	_____
Pitch 7	M (0)	LD (7–10)	FB (0–7)	GB (0–7)	_____
Pitch 8	M (0)	LD (7–10)	FB (0–7)	GB (0–7)	_____
Pitch 9	M (0)	LD (7–10)	FB (0–7)	GB (0–7)	_____
Pitch 10	M (0)	LD (7–10)	FB (0–7)	GB (0–7)	_____

Subtotal _____*

Divide this subtotal by 2 and enter number on Total line.

Total: _____ of 50

Hitting Quotient (H.Q.)

To determine the rating, or final score, of the batter, add the scores for each of the sections (Part 1, Part 2, and Parts 3A, 3B, and 3C).

Part 1   _____ of 10
Part 2   _____ of 10
Part 3A   _____ of 20
Part 3B   _____ of 10
Part 3C   _____ of 50

Final Grade or H.Q.: _____ of *100* (*maximum score*)

(Circle one)

Grade of 75 to 100	Hall of Famer
Grade of 65 to 74	All Star
Grade of 50 to 64	Major league player
Grade of 49 or less	AAA player

Comments: _____

_____

Evaluator: _____   Date: _____
(signature)

Index

123